S0-FKK-513

CASES IN MANAGEMENT

Examining Critical Incidents

CASES IN MANAGEMENT

Examining Critical Incidents

D. Neil Ashworth
E. Claiborne Robins School of Business
University of Richmond, Virginia

Reston Publishing Company, Inc.
A Prentice-Hall Company
Reston, Virginia

Property of Library
Cape Fear Technical Institute
Wilmington, N. C.

Library of Congress Cataloging in Publication Data
Ashworth, D. Neil.
    Cases in management.
    1. Organizational behavior—Case studies.
2. Management—Case studies.   I. Title.
HD58.7.A89   1985   658   84–18123
ISBN 0-8359-0706-6

Production supervision/interior design: Tally Morgan

© 1985 by Reston Publishing Company, Inc.
A Prentice-Hall Company
Reston, Virginia 22090

All rights reserved. No part of this book may be
reproduced in any way, or by any means, without
permission in writing from the publisher.

10 9 8 7 6 5 4 3 2 1

Printed in the United States of America

TO MARLENE

CONTENTS

CASES

Topical coverage of management functions, activities, and responsibilities

Case	Atti-tude	Communi-cation	Conflict	Control-ling	Leader-ship	Motiva-tion	Organ. change & dev.	Organ. climate	Organ. structure & design	Planning	Stress
1		X	X		X						
2	X		X		X	X					
3			X	X							X
4				X				X		X	
5		X	X		X	X			X	X	
6		X				X	X			X	
7	X					X		X			
8		X			X				X		X
9	X					X	X			X	X
10					X					X	
11		X								X	
12	X		X		X					X	
13		X	X			X	X				
14	X	X		X	X						
15			X	X			X				
16	X				X		X				
17				X						X	X
18		X			X		X				
19		X			X	X					X
20	X					X					
21			X					X	X		
22	X				X	X	X	X	X	X	
23					X			X		X	
24			X	X	X						
25	X			X	X		X				
26						X	X		X		
27		X			X		X				
28		X	X								
29	X	X	X								
30		X			X	X	X				X
31		X			X		X			X	
32		X							X		
33			X								
34		X	X		X	X					
35		X	X		X	X					X
36			X			X				X	

PREFACE

Cases in Management: Examining Critical Incidents was written to provide students with an opportunity to apply basic concepts normally taught in management and organizational behavior courses. Past experiences in the classroom suggest greater student appreciation and understanding of organization concepts such as planning, leadership, and group dynamics if they can be applied to a "real world" setting. The cases contained in this text offer a variety of organization settings as the backdrop for analysis and discussion of such concepts. It may be appropriate to use this book as the primary text in a management case course or as a supplemental text in a more structured management or organizational behavior course.

A great deal of credit for the development of this text can be given to several members of the local business community who were part-time students in our graduate program in business. These individuals were asked to closely examine their current (or previous) organizations and provide evidence of neglect for sound management practices. Their observations were recorded in the form of cases or background material for cases. It is through their experiences that students have that actual business setting previously noted.

I would like to recognize those individuals who were sensitive to and supportive of my objectives by sharing their experiences: Corby Bailey, Preston Walters, John Blatecky, Henry Seaman, Lowndes Burke, Mary Anne Burke, June Deyerle, Donna Myers, Louie Love, David Boor, Betsy Wilton, Rodger Rhinehart, John Krovic, Charles Grant, Janet Cousins, Mark Pearce, John McCarthy, Jr., Jim Smith, Howard Kaplan, Ed Wiles, Harvey Neale, Bob Wetzel, Fred Cousins, Diane Doyle, Brett Paladino, Richard Brandt, Marie Robertson, Cindy O'Berry, Laddie Bell, Joe Moynihan, Patty Mears, Reverdy Howley, Joe Ross, Tom Manter, Roy Carpenter, and Walt Riggs.

The invaluable contributions of these individuals should not be understated. However, except as noted, their acknowledgment is restricted to *this* portion of the text. This was done solely to protect the innocent (and, unfortunately, the guilty) members of the various organizations. Moreover, while the incidents depicted in the cases are factual, the names of the organizations and their principal characters have been disguised to ensure even greater anonymity.

There are many others who also deserve recognition for making this project a reality. Initially, I would like to thank Bruce Meglino of the University of South Carolina who has served as mentor, role model, and friend. Without his efforts, I would not have felt prepared to undertake this project. I would also like to acknowledge the assistance offered by my colleagues in the University of Richmond's E. Claiborne Robins School of Business with special thanks to the following: Ken Matejka, who gave me my "jump start" and provided encouragement along the way; Dave Ekey for his understanding and support; and Dean Thomas L. Reuschling for his appreciation and support for my goals. Special thanks is also due to a number of individuals at Reston Publishing Company: Bob Dame for his support during the project's inception; Catherine Rossbach for her ideas, support, and patience throughout the course of the project; and the technical assistance provided by Tally Morgan and Karen Winget.

A great deal of appreciation is likewise extended to those who graciously accepted the task of typing the manuscript: Mrs. Shirley Fisk for her help during the introductory chapters; Miss Jane Starkey for her assistance with eleventh-hour additions and corrections; and Mrs. Mary Anne Wilbourne whose patience, typing, and editing skills throughout the entire project cannot be adequately recognized in such a short space.

Finally, this list of acknowledgments would be incomplete if I did not recognize the patience, moral support, and encouragement of my wife, Marlene, throughout this project. Her love and devotion made all of the challenges easier to confront.

CASES IN MANAGEMENT

Examining Critical Incidents

CHAPTER ONE:
AN OVERVIEW
OF MANAGEMENT

Whereas most people have their own ideas of what constitutes the management process, it is probably safe to say that the descriptions are often too limited in their scope; that is, many would suggest that management is simply telling *people* what to do on the job. Although generating orders is certainly part of a manager's role, such a description does not begin to reveal the complexity of the management process. Consequently, in order to establish some consensus regarding this process, we will subscribe to the following definition of management:

> Management is a process of planning, organizing, actuating, and controlling an organization's operations in order to achieve a coordination of the human and material resources essential in the effective and efficient attainment of objectives.[1]

This definition proposes that the management process is multifaceted and dynamic in nature and is absolutely essential in moving an organization toward its goals and objectives. Because of the complexity of our definition, however, it is beneficial to examine the components of the management process in greater detail.

[1]R. L. Trewatha and M. G. Newport, *Management*, Third Edition (Plano, TX: Business Publications, Inc., 1982), p. 5.

THE MULTIFUNCTIONALITY OF MANAGEMENT

All managers at all levels of an organization are involved in numerous functions such as planning. However, the emphasis placed on each function varies according to the position the manager holds within the organization. For example, upper-level management will typically be concerned with long-range planning (10 years) while the short-run or operational planning (a year or less) will be a responsibility of lower-level, supervisory management personnel. The degree of preoccupation with any of the managerial functions noted in the definition will differ on the basis of hierarchical position.

Planning

The managerial function of planning has been defined as "the process of using related facts and future assumptions to arrive at courses of action to be followed in seeking specific goals."[2] Planning is critical for the organization since it provides direction and, most important, forces the organization to forecast its environment rather than take a wait-and-see attitude.[3]

Preparation for the planning process will typically involve an appraisal of both the internal and external environments of an organization. Such an appraisal is followed by an analysis of proposed plans in light of the

[2]Trewatha and Newport, p. 74.

[3]M. A. Hitt, R. D. Middlemist, and R. L. Mathis, *Effective Management* (St. Paul, MN: West Publishing Co., 1979), p. 12.

4

strengths and weaknesses of the firm and the potential opportunities and risks created by the plans.

Though planning is but one of the many managerial functions, it may be the most important and thus require the most attention. It is a starting point for all managers and precedes the need for the organizing, leading, and controlling functions. Consequently, though the functions presented here may suggest a particular sequence of action, this may not be the case except with respect to planning. Without plans and the policies that grow out of the plans, there is an insurmountable obstacle to carrying out the remaining functions.

Organizing

The function of organizing has been defined as "the process of arranging people and physical resources in order to carry out plans."[4] Organizing is essential in a firm's efforts to achieve a synergistic effect among its many departments and groups. Specifically, the manager is responsible for arranging the resources—both human and physical—in such a manner that the whole (total output) is greater than the sum of the individual parts.

Organizing occurs on both a vertical and horizontal basis within the firm. Vertical coordination involves a clarification of the relationships between superiors and subordinates throughout the firm. Among the activities are determining who has been granted formal authority, deciding when delegation of authority may

[4]L. E. Boone and D. L. Kurtz, *Principles of Management* (New York: Random House, 1981), p. 123.

be necessary, and creating a functional span of control within the firm. Equally important and perhaps more difficult than vertical coordination is a manager's concern for organizing individuals at the same levels within the firm. Such horizontal coordination is critical because the firm's activities (sales, accounting, shipping, for example) are divided among groups that must work together in order to produce the final product or service.

The complexity of the organizing process will not be the same for all firms. How difficult it will be for a manager to create an efficient organization structure will depend on such factors as the size of the firm, the abilities of employees, and how much decentralization is required or desired for maximum efficiency of operations. Regardless of complexity, the organizing function is necessary for the successful movement toward the plans established by management.

Actuating

In addition to planning and organizing, a manager must be capable of initiating and directing the work in an organization. This function is described as actuating and includes motivation, leadership, communication, training, and other forms of personal influence.[5]

The contemporary manager is becoming increasingly aware that individuals behave differently from each other and therefore are not necessarily motivated in the same manner. All employees are not motivated by the same rewards, and it is a manager's responsibility to recognize the different employee preferences

[5]Trewatha and Newport, p. 7.

for the rewards offered by the organization. For example, there are many employees who are highly motivated to perform better for monetary rewards and care little or nothing for other inducements such as offices, secretaries, and recognition. Conversely, there are employees who desire monetary rewards but also have a strong desire for a quality worklife. It is a manager's job to recognize an employee's needs and attempt to satisfy these needs as an inducement to performance improvement.

The ability to direct or lead is one of the more recognized activities of a manager. The degree of leadership effectiveness achieved by managers generally depends on a number of factors, including individual traits and personality, the nature of the task (e.g., routine/structured versus nonroutine/unstructured), and acceptance by the followers.

Many individuals argue that the true source of leadership is the respect earned from those being led. Moreover, that it is the role of the individual rather than the individual himself or herself that requires acceptance. There are individuals who lead successfully because they are respected for their ability to get the job done even though they may not be well liked.

Numerous theories of leadership have been proposed over the years, and many have attempted to establish a universal prescription for effective leadership.[6] Most contemporary theories, however, have focused on a *contingency* approach. With this perspective, an effective style of leadership depends on such

[6]For greater detail on the numerous leadership theories, see for example, John B. Miner, *Theories of Organizational Behavior* (Hinsdale, IL: Dryden Press, 1980), pp. 267–388 or J. L. Gibson, J. M. Ivancevich, and J. H. Donnelly, Jr., *Organizations*, Fourth Edition (Plano, TX: Business Publications, Inc., 1982), pp. 228–277.

factors as the degree of authority delegated to the manager, the type of needs expressed by the followers, and the complexity of the task. That is, a leader's particular style may not be effective in all situations or with all individuals.

A major part of the actuating function is the ability to communicate effectively with other members of the organization. All managerial functions noted thus far cannot be carried out without the use of some form of communication. Therefore, a manager must be able to recognize the common barriers to effective communication such as distortion, information overload, jargon, and an individual's frame of reference. More importantly, the manager must be able to overcome such barriers by showing empathy (being receiver-oriented), repeating messages for greater clarity, and regulating the flow of information that is passed on to others. In general, then, a manager must be able to get his or her message across to others as intended in order to carry out plans, organize, motivate, and lead with optimal effectiveness.

Controlling

Controls are established within the organization to ensure the compliance of activities with the plans, orders, and objectives that have been initiated by management. The control process typically involves a series of distinct sequential steps:[7]

1. Determine performance standards.

2. Measure actual performance.

[7]See Hitt *et al.*, p. 342 and Trewatha and Newport, pp. 434–439.

3. Compare actual versus desired performance.

4. Evaluate the deviations.

5. Implement corrective action (if necessary) or reward good performance.

In the course of establishing controls, management must make sure that the controls are economical and timely in order to be effective. In other words, the costs of implementing and maintaining controls should not be greater than the costs of having no controls at all. For example, you would most likely not install a time clock if only one or two employees occasionally come into work five minutes late. In addition, the controls must provide immediate performance feedback to enable a manager to make adjustments that may be necessary while work is in process.

Managers should also be aware that implementing controls can place unintended constraints on individual workers. Specifically, controls may restrict individual creativity and therefore generate attitudinal problems or possible conflict both within and between task groups. In general, a manager must recognize the value of an efficient control system within the organization but must employ the controls in such a manner that they will be seen as beneficial by individual workers, not as constraints.

SUMMARY

It is extremely difficult to do justice to the multidimensional role of today's manager in such a short space. However, the point has been established that effective management is a complex process involving a multitude of activities. We have examined but a few points here.

More than anything else, you should realize that management is not a discipline that is separate and distinct from marketing, production, finance, or accounting. In reality, those individuals seeking to rise within an organization's hierarchy will generally find themselves managing more and more people and materials as they progress. Therefore, a fundamental understanding of management is essential for today's business student regardless of specific career interests. This book is intended to place you in a situation of examining actual business problems and, more importantly, generating potential solutions. Although you may face situations that differ in some respects from the specific situations presented here, the cases will encourage you to take a more analytical approach to the problems examined.

ADDITIONAL RESOURCES ON THE MANAGEMENT PROCESS

Albanese, Robert. *Managing Toward Accountability for Performance*, 3rd Ed. Homewood, Il: Richard D. Irwin, Inc., 1981.

Dessler, Gary. *Management Fundamentals*, 3rd Ed. Reston, VA: Reston Publishing Company, 1982.

Donnelly, James H., Jr., Gibson, James L., and Ivancevich, John M. *Fundamentals of Management*, 4th Ed. Plano, TX: Business Publications, Inc., 1981.

Hampton, David R. *Contemporary Management*, 2nd Ed. New York: McGraw-Hill, Inc., 1981.

Huse, Edgar F. *Management,* 2nd Ed. St. Paul: West
    Publishing, 1982.
Koontz, Harold, O'Donnell, Cyril, and Weihrich, Heinz.
    Management, 7th Ed. New York: McGraw-Hill,
    Inc., 1980.
Longenecker, Justin G., and Pringle, Charles D. *Man-
    agement,* 5th Ed. Columbus, OH: Charles E. Mer-
    rill Publishing Company, 1981.
Mescon, Michael H., Albert, Michael, and Khedouri,
    Franklin. *Management.* New York: Harper & Row,
    1981.
Szilagyi, Andrew D., Jr. *Management and Perform-
    ance.* Santa Monica, CA: Goodyear Publishing
    Company, 1981.

CHAPTER TWO:
THE CASE
ANALYSIS PROCESS

In preparation for problems that may be encountered in the business world, you are encouraged to become more familiar with the case analysis process.[1] The approach offers hands-on experience regarding the complexities of human interaction on the individual, group, and organization level. Fortunately, the price paid for an error in organizational analysis while in the classroom is usually much less than the price paid in the business world.

In general, the case provides us with an organizational situation or incident that requires in-depth analysis. The problems within the organization may be concerned with such managerial functions as planning or organizing. However, it is also possible that the problems may deal with such subjective factors as leadership style, motivation of subordinates, or ability to communicate with various levels in the organizational hierarchy.

An important consideration in using the case method, however, is that cases are typically situation-specific. Therefore, a recommended solution for any particular case may not be applicable to cases involving other groups or organizations even when most of the factors are similar. The principal contribution of the case method is to induce careful, systematic analysis of critical incidents that may occur in any type of organization or group. If you are capable of identifying prob-

[1]For detailed coverage of the case approach, readers are advised to see *The Business Case Method: An Introduction* by J. Kenneth Matejka and Thomas J. Cosse (Reston Publishing Company, 1981).

lems and solutions for one firm, then it is possible that the same *analytical process* can be applied to other case situations.

STEPS IN THE CASE ANALYSIS

The actual case analysis involves a number of sequential steps. Each of these steps is intended to bring you closer to a problem solution while considering the numerous factors relevant to the case. Although there does not appear to be universal agreement on the exact number of steps involved, the content is fairly consistent among all sources. Each of these steps should be considered individually in order to demonstrate a logical flow from problem definition to solution.

Step One: Determine the Problem(s)

Once a case has been reviewed several times, it is necessary to recognize (and study) the problems that appear to exist. The important aspect of this step is determining whether a particular problem is, in fact, a problem or a *symptom* of the real problem. As a case in point, consider the employee who is consistently late for work in the morning and whose performance has steadily declined over the past six months. Is the problem tardiness? Can tardiness lead to declining performance because of less time on the job? Or is the tardiness the result of other factors, such as a motivational problem that has not been addressed or riding in a carpool with a driver who is late?

In general, determination of problems invariably requires going beneath the surface of the case to uncover factors that are relevant but not obvious in a casual review. Very rarely (if at all) will the problems in a case jump off the page. Therefore, you are urged to undertake an extensive deliberation of all factors while focusing on the problem areas in a case.

Step Two: Determine Alternative Courses of Action

Once the problems in a case have been determined, it is necessary to examine alternative courses of action that will hopefully enable you to resolve the problems. During this step, there is typically a great deal of brainstorming in an attempt to account for as many alternatives as possible. Obviously not all alternative courses of action will be equally viable, but each may generate some additional considerations. Remember, you are merely trying to create as many alternatives as possible without assessing the merits of each.

Step Three: Evaluate Alternative Courses of Action

After generating potential alternative courses of action, it is necessary to examine the strengths and weaknesses of *each* alternative. Some alternatives will obviously have more merits (and fewer weaknesses) than others, but the main point is to determine the alternative that addresses the case problem with respect to both the short and long run. It is critical that the student consider all the consequences of each alternative, because what may seem to be the obvious course of action now may lead to dysfunctional effects in the future.

Step Four: Select and Defend Alternatives

After weighing the pros and cons of each alternative, it is then necessary to select the alternative that has emerged as the most attractive course of action for dealing with the particular problems at hand. It is important that you have the factual ammunition that will enable you to defend your choice of alternatives.

A major concern during this stage of the process is that your final choice may not be perceived as the best by others who are analyzing the case. This is not totally unexpected since not *all* the facts are available in cases, and we must rely on our inferences when arriving at a final decision. Since everybody is different in some respects, it is not unusual for several people to make different inferences regarding the same case.

Step Five: Implement Selected Alternative(s)

The case analysis process is not concluded until a suitable plan has been developed for implementing the selected course of action. Improper implementation will negate the time and effort spent up to this point. To illustrate, consider a decision made by the Postal

Service to upgrade its technology in order to handle and deliver mail more efficiently. After extensive deliberation regarding available funds, the decision is made to purchase new equipment, but allocation of funds for maintenance of delivery vehicles is not even discussed!

We may even go as far as suggesting that a poor plan properly implemented may be better than a good plan that does not address the implementation issue. This may be especially true concerning the involvement of those individuals implementing the final decision. Their involvement and commitment is critical to success.

FINAL CONSIDERATION

Although case analysis offers a careful, systematic method of dealing with an organization's problems, it is not without shortcomings. Recognition and understanding of the potential obstacles encountered during the process is necessary in order to complete the process in an effective manner.

Initially, you are advised (again) to closely scrutinize a case prior to engaging in the suggested step procedure. By doing so, identification of problems is facilitated, and the time that may be inadvertently spent on symptoms of problems is decreased. It has often been stated that a problem well defined is half solved.

In addition, be aware of the difference in opinion that may arise regarding the choice of alternative courses of action. As noted previously, not everybody will see a case situation exactly as you see it. Therefore, there is likely to be a difference of opinion regardless of the case being examined or the alternative selected. To cope with this situation, you must be open minded. It is not always possible for you to have the best course of action relative to others. However, by carefully preparing for a case discussion and being able to listen effectively to others, you are likely to enhance your analytical skills and objectivity in the long run.

A final comment deals with the concept of the case study itself. As an organization research tool, the case study is attractive because information (data) regarding an individual, group, or organization is already present and does not have to be obtained by more empirical methods (e.g., field experiment or field survey). Therefore, the case method is relatively inexpensive and quick. The cost of this convenience, however, is that the information contained in a case is typically based on someone's perception or inferences regarding the situations taking place in some firm. Consequently, an appraisal of the perceived problems within an organization may not be as objective as desired.

In conclusion, case analysis can be a valuable tool if used properly. The case is intended to eliminate a shallow, rule-of-thumb approach to problem solving in favor of a systematic, analytical examination process. If you can see the logic behind the step process and understand the problems that may arise during the process, *then* you are ready to begin your analysis of the cases that have been provided.

1

MID-ATLANTIC COLD SODA, INC.

Carl Abell was looking forward to the weekend. It had been a terribly hectic week, and if this morning's staff meeting was any indication, next week would be just as bad. In order to achieve the deadlines set for his department, Carl would have to give an extra push to his staff, which was already short one person and stretched to the limit by the last three months of overtime. But now, at four o'clock on Friday afternoon, Carl was thinking about the plans he and his wife had made for the weekend when two of his employees, engaged in a bitter argument, entered his office.

This was not the first time that Bill Cardin, the accounting supervisor, and Jim Marlow, a staff accountant, had been involved in a dispute. In fact, Carl had noticed a great deal of tension in the whole department lately, which he attributed to the long period of overtime. After hearing the two men argue for a few minutes, Carl stopped them, saying, "Look, fellas, it's Friday night. Can't this wait until Monday morning? Maybe by then you will both have cooled down and we can talk it over reasonably." Both men seemed reluctant to let the issue drop, but seeing that Carl was unwilling to listen to them, they left his office glaring at each other, and at Carl.

Driving home that night, Carl reflected on his year as manager of accounting for Mid-Atlantic Cold Soda, Inc., a bottler and distributor of several major brands of soft drinks. The company, which serves parts of Virginia, Maryland, Pennsylvania, and the District of Columbia, had been formed by a group of investors who consolidated several smaller franchises into the present corporate structure. It had been in existence for only 18 months prior to the time Carl accepted his position and moved his family from New York, where he had earned his MBA degree and had gained most of his work experience, first for a major public accounting firm and then in various management positions for a large textile manufacturer. Carl had encountered many problems during the past year, most of which he had been able to resolve satisfactorily through his commitment to the job, the sacrifice of much of his leisure time, and the motivation of his staff. But one problem he had been unable to solve was the dissension and conflict among the members of the department, a problem that was beginning to show in their work.

Upon arriving home, Carl resolved not to let the problem spoil his weekend, but during dinner he found himself thinking again about that afternoon's incident. Despite his usual policy of not bringing work-related problems home, he was relieved when his wife asked him what was wrong. The following conversation took place.

Carl: Bill and Jim had an argument today just before we left work. I told them to cool off and come see me Monday morning, because I didn't want them to say anything they would regret later. They're both good workers and I can't afford to lose either one of them, especially right now when we're already short-handed.

Wife: What were they arguing about?

Carl: I never did find out. But lately everyone seems to be on edge. I don't understand it. When I promoted Bill instead of going outside the company to fill the supervisor's position, I thought everyone would be pleased and support Bill. I needed someone with his experience in the bottling industry to show me the ropes, and Bill had been there the longest. Anyway, if I hadn't promoted him, I probably would have lost him to another company by now.

Wife: Has he ever had a job supervising people before? When I met him at the company picnic he seemed young for a job with that much responsibility.

Carl: Well, this is his only job since graduation from college, but I'm sure he can handle it. He has made a few mistakes in dealing with his employees that have caused problems, and some people find his ways a little abrasive at times. But I personally have no complaints. He gets the job done and he's very loyal to me. He just needs some more time to get used to his new job.

Leaving it at that, Carl turned the conversation to their plans for the rest of the weekend. But several times during the weekend his thoughts returned to the problem, until he decided what he would do. Arriving at work Monday morning, he called Bill into his office and the following exchange took place.

Carl: Suppose you tell me what happened between you and Jim last Friday.

Bill: All I did was ask Jim for a copy of some reimbursement requests he was supposed to have filed for our TV and radio expenditures. He gave me a funny look and told me that he hadn't had time to prepare them. When I asked him why, he blew up and started yelling at me. That's when I brought him into your office. Carl, I told him two weeks ago to prepare those requests as soon as possible. If we don't get them filed soon the company will lose money. George in advertising has been on my back to send them off, and last week I told him that we had. I can't do my job properly if these people won't do what I tell them to.

Carl: I know I've been asking a lot from you lately, Bill, and I want you to know that knowing that I can depend on you has been a big help to me. I haven't been able to spend much time with you in the three months since your promotion. But as soon as these interviews are over and we're back to full staff, we'll sit down together and see if we can find some way to reorganize the workload and eliminate the overtime. Everyone is just tired and on edge right now, including you and me. Hang in there for a few more weeks and things will get better.

Bill: I'll try. I just hope these people start to realize that I'm their supervisor now. Otherwise there's going to be more trouble.

Carl: Don't worry, Bill. I'll talk to Jim about it.

Bill left the office and Carl then asked Jim to step into his office for a few minutes. Jim entered the office still obviously angry about the past week's incident and a little surprised not to find Bill there. Carl asked him to sit down and then explained the reasons for the visit.

Carl: Jim, I thought that since you and Bill are still upset about last week, it would be best if I talked to you separately. Maybe we can avoid a repeat of last Friday's incident. Why don't you tell me what happened?

Jim: Okay. Bill gave me some reimbursement forms to fill out about a week ago and told me to work on them when I had time. Then last Friday he came looking for them. When I told him I hadn't completed them yet he gave me one of those sarcastic looks of his and yelled "Why not?" That's when I lost my temper and we ended up in your office. Carl, he should know why I haven't finished those forms. He's given me half a dozen things since then that all had to be done "right away" according to him. I've only got two hands, you know! I didn't mind taking on an extra load temporarily when Ken resigned, because I knew you were in a bind. But I just can't do any more. Doesn't Bill understand that? I already work nights, and I've been taking things home on weekends to keep up with my regular work. I'm fed up with his insinuations that I don't work hard enough. Everyone else in the department has just about had it with him, too. If Bill doesn't back off, you are going to lose some more people before you are through.

Carl: Jim, I appreciate the extra work you've been doing, and so does Bill. He's been putting a lot of pressure on himself to do well since his promotion and he needs a little more time to adjust to his new responsibilities. I'll speak to him about getting you some help with those requests. Meanwhile, try to hang in there. The overtime won't last much longer.

Jim: Thanks, Carl, I'm glad to know that *someone* around here still appreciates me!

QUESTIONS

1. Do you agree with the way Carl Abell handled the situation? Was he right to delay the confrontation between Jim and Bill?

2. Jim's version of the incidents leading up to the confrontation varies greatly from that of Bill. What communications problems appear to have contributed to the disagreement? How could these problems have been avoided?

3. Do you agree with Carl that the main cause of the problem is the excessive overtime? Based on Jim's remarks, can Carl expect more problems in the future?

2

BODINE ELECTRONICS

Bodine Electronics was created in the early 1950s in the garage of Ted Bodine. Initially work was done at nights and on weekends while Ted was still working full-time for Apex Systems, Inc., a leading electronic connector company. Ted decided to start his own firm because of opportunities created by Apex's refusal to bid on a number of special custom requests by its customers.

By 1968, Bodine Electronics, along with the booming connector industry, had greatly expanded to reach a sales level of $17 million. In 1968, Rufus Chemical approached Bodine with a request for a highly technical connector apparatus, and Bodine responded excellently, from an initial concept to delivering a final product ahead of schedule. Rufus, a chemical industry giant, had been continuously on the watch for acquisitions in high-growth industries to diversify from the competitive chemical industry. Thus, in 1972, Rufus acquired Bodine Electronics for $25 million and retained Ted Bodine as a consultant for one year.

The primary reason Ted Bodine sold the company to Rufus was because the excessive growth of his company had become unmanageable. The old days of walking across the hall to discuss an application problem with the chief engineer were gone. Hundreds of people were now employed at Bodine, and internal communications were becoming a real problem. Ted would complain, "The left hand doesn't know what the right hand is doing anymore."

One reason Bodine Electronics grew so fast (25-40 percent per year) was that the electronics industry itself was on a roll; everything was going electronic. Banking machines, computers, microwave ovens, copiers, televisions, printers, and hundreds of other products required the use of connectors. As these industries grew, the connector industry grew right along with them.

THE SALES ORGANIZATION TODAY

The Bodine Electronics Division of Rufus Chemical Corporation currently employs approximately 150 sales engineers to cover the United States and Canada. Sales engineers are paid a straight salary. Unlike other companies in the electronics industry, Rufus offers no commission or incentive plan. However, Rufus is well known for an outstanding fringe benefits package.

The sales force at Bodine is generally well respected and talented. It is a strong organization, known for its ability to carry the division even through hard economic times. In this fiscal year, however, the sales force was slipping in performance, earnings were declining to all-time lows, and the pressure from Rufus corporate headquarters was beginning to bear down.

The sales department generally had recruited young technical- or business-oriented college graduates. Once hired, they entered the Bodine Sales Training Program, which was a 6-10 month intensive training schedule consisting of detailed product familiarization and training in selling approaches and techniques.

The Attitude Problem

Ben Billings, national sales manager, summed it up best at the sales managers' meeting in February: "I've noticed a continuing decline in positive attitude from many of our sales engineers, particularly the newer, younger salesmen who have been with the company less than five years. I believe this decline in attitude is affecting performance, both individual and company. I expect all the district managers to find out what the problem is and to recommend alternative solutions. Report back to me by March 15."

As the meeting ended, south central district manager Dave Simmons asked Wilbur Cassle, north central district manager, to join him for a stiff drink in the hotel lounge. "Sure, Dave, I can use one after that meeting."

"I don't know, Wilbur. Lately, whenever I hold a district sales meeting, it turns into a complaining session: all negative comments from my salesmen."

"Same here, Dave. You would think these guys aren't even getting paid to do the job. Rufus is one of the best paying, great benefit companies around. Those salesmen don't realize how fortunate they are."

During the following week, Dave Simmons wasted no time in getting feedback from his sales engineers. He called a district meeting for all of his subordinates to meet in the office for a full workday. The following exchange took place:

Dave: OK folks. Sales are down. Profits are down. Enthusiasm is down. I want to know why. What are the problems? What is keeping us from achieving our sales goals?

Bucky: I'll tell you, Dave. It's a little tough to sell something we don't have. Those bums in the product marketing department are who to blame! In the past three years, 21 new products were introduced to the field and only two made it to the market on time. We go out pushing these new products only to find out there are none in stock.

Tom: That's right! And then we get 16 weeks delivery time to quote a customer.

Bev: This kind of thing hurts our credibility with the customers. We promise we'll have a certain new product by a certain time, and it never happens.

Jim: What makes me mad is that we are forced to include these new products in our forecasted sales plan each year. Often the product has not yet been completed but we have to forecast sales of it anyway. Later, if that new product never makes it to the market, I've committed to sell, let's say, $100 M worth. Now, I've got to scramble around and find that business elsewhere!

Woody: Yeah! How come we can always "revise" our sales quotas upward based on new information, but never downward?

Jim: Our job performance is directly affected by those turkeys in product marketing. I could do my job 150 percent, but if marketing doesn't get these new products out the door, I still have to sell an equal dollar amount in existing products! There's only so much business out there for mature product lines.

Tom: And when job performance is negatively affected, so is my salary increase! That's not fair! I am dependent on the product marketing group and when they don't come through, I fall short of my quota and get a measly percentage increase at the end of the year, if I'm lucky.

Sam: I'm not surprised at all. We have to rely on a bunch of hot-shot MBA'ers, who have little or no field sales experience. They are not customer-oriented. They don't understand the critical importance of timing and responsiveness.

Chuck: Those product marketing clowns are one issue, but another reason we're behind our year-to-date goals is because they were set too high in the first place. This MBO (Management by Objective) program we introduced two years ago is a real joke! Management tells us we can set our own goals. But management already has a predetermined goal dictated from corporate headquarters. If our individual forecasts don't total high enough, management raises our goals for us! That's some democratic participation!

Bev: And management always sets the goals too high. They're not based on real customer opportunities; more often than not, they're gung ho, pie-in-the-sky forecasts designed to impress somebody! Our performance would be much better right now if we had stuck with our original forecasts. They were realistic.

Tom: If we could get a bonus or commission instead of just straight salary, it might be easier to put up with all the abuse we take out there.

Jim: I don't know, Tom. Being on commission would make us even more dependent on our product marketing department. We'd really be at their throats if our weekly bread and butter depended on them.

Bucky: I agree with Tom. There's no incentive to sell more than our annual quota. If I do 100 percent of goal or 150 percent of goal I get about the same level of salary increase. Why should I get ulcers and bust my hump when I don't get compensated for it!

Rob: I don't see what all the fuss is about. Sales are down because we are in a recession. Customers are laying off people, shutting down plants, working reduced workweeks, etc. There's not much we can do until the economy picks up.

Sam: What amazes me is that we always seem to be the last company to enter the market with a new product. All we get from marketing after all the delays is a "me, too" product. I've been in this business for 18 years and I'm telling you, time and time again, we arrive three to five years too late with our new product introductions. By that time, our customers are asking for something else that Apex or another competitor is offering. By the time one of our new products is finally introduced, some of us have had so many disappointments we've lost confidence in it.

In this electronics industry, the average product life cycle lasts five years, then new technology hits the market. We must adapt to the fast pace of this industry in all phases of management.

Rudy: I'm confused with what you really expect us salesmen to do. Too much emphasis is placed on making a lot of sales calls each day, with little regard to making fewer, good quality, qualified calls. You want us to plan and organize our territories better, but that takes time. If we're on the road all the time, we cannot plan, except for nights and weekends. But there's no time to do all the follow-up work required during business hours to really service our key accounts.

Tom: Too often we're caught in the middle: we have to side with our customers and also with Bodine. But when Bodine's product marketing or other departments injure our reputation with my customers, I get blamed, even though I have no formal authority to direct the decisions of these groups.

Dave: OK, I've heard enough. That's all for today.

After everyone had left, Dave sat alone in his office and wondered what alternative courses of action he would recommend to Ben Billings as corrective measures to cure the sales slump and the negative attitudes expressed by the sales force.

QUESTIONS

1. Based on the dialogue, what are the major factors contributing to the decline in motivation of Dave Simmons' sales force?
2. What approaches (if any) could Dave Simmons take to resolve the apparent conflict between his sales force and the product marketing department?

3

CHEMSERVICES, INC.

Meredith Marshall is the 30-year-old district accountant for Chemservices, Inc., a midwestern-based corporation that services small and large institutions and corporations for solid waste removal. Located in Maryland, Meredith's district is part of one division that services manufacturing and utility companies for chemical cleaning and hydroblasting. This division of Chemservices has been steadily losing money for the past five years and is the only division that is not in the solid waste service. Although the chemical cleaning division has been in the red on a consolidated basis, the Maryland district for the past three years has had earnings of 20 percent of gross sales and leads the division with a high return on investment.

Chemservices was started in 1962 by Daniel Winters, who began his corporation with a single refuse truck, servicing his local residential area. Through a policy of rapid expansion and tight management policies and controls, by 1972 Chemservices was the leader in solid waste removal for the east coast. As positive expansion continued with the purchase of small local refuse companies, Chemservices began to purchase local chemical cleaning and hydroblasting companies in addition to solid waste removal firms. Upper management felt that by purchasing these chemical service companies they could provide their large customers with additional services, thus strengthening their already strong business ties. In 1975, Chemservices had a total of 18 service locations throughout the continental United States and Puerto Rico.

At the time of the acquisitions of the various chemical service companies, very few new personnel were hired who had specific technical knowledge of this particular service. Various selected individuals at the different locations stayed on with Chemservices during the consolidation, and the open sales, marketing, and service slots were filled with transfers from the solid waste division. As time progressed, sales and profits decreased with customers lost to competitors because of the declining quality and the stagnant variety of services performed.

At the end of fiscal 1981, upper management of Chemservices decided to give the chemical cleaning division its full attention, with the goal of turning around the losing division. New district personnel were hired in many instances with an emphasis on obtaining employees with knowledge of chemical cleaning. In addition, new tight management policies and restrictions were implemented. Fiscal 1982 was designated the "year of the cleanup," and management expected 1983 to show a break-even status. The majority of new policies was directed at controlling costs and standardizing accounting procedures. These policies, however, were written by headquarter-based personnel whose backgrounds were in the solid waste area, and the new procedures did not always address the problems associated with the chemical cleaning business. Often they generated additional paperwork and problems because they were at odds with the nature of the business.

When Meredith interviewed with John Grey and then accepted the district accountant position in September, 1981, a tight economic and job condition prevailed in Maryland. Although her skills and previous job references were excellent, she had been unemployed for over a year. After the death of her father and upon persistent pressure from her husband, she had worked as a temporary accountant during the summer until the job market had become less restrictive. When contemplating whether or not to accept the position as offered, she knew that the small and noisy office atmosphere might be a problem to her after working in deluxe offices for a bank, but the laid-back and relaxed attitude of John Grey, her future boss, would be an asset.

John Grey, the district manager, was a quiet man with a ready smile and a subdued personality. He told her that she would report to him only and that she would be supervising a total of three office staff. She would have the total reporting responsibility of all accounting at the district level. In addition, he stated that whatever she wanted to do was all right with him.

After accepting the position at a salary somewhat less than she desired, she met with her accounting staff. Rosa Cartland, the accounts payable and insurance clerk, was an attractive woman in her mid-40s. Compulsive and highly critical by nature, she took valium to calm her nerves and make her job more bearable. Although extremely moody and adverse to change, her performance of those tasks assigned was excellent. Josie Perkins, 42, was the part-time payroll and accounts receivable clerk. Fun-loving and a gossip, she had a hard time learning the assigned tasks. However, if no problems arose, her job duties were carried out in a proficient manner. Even though she worked only part-time hours and was hired a year after Rosa, John hired Josie at 55¢ per hour more than Rosa. The receptionist/secretary/invoice clerk was Dora Olin, an older attractive woman with a pleasant manner. Although she tackled her assigned duties with a positive attitude, unlike Rosa, she often forgot details and tuned out instructions and information. If criticized, on a rare occasion, her feelings were sensitive and easily hurt. Rosa did not like Dora and criticized her work to those outside the department, and Dora felt that Rosa was overly critical and cold-natured. Eventually all unnecessary communication and conversation ceased between the two.

At the fiscal year-end close of 1981 in September, immediate changes began to take place. In addition to the flood of new procedures and special projects, Carol Smithfield was appointed as assistant divisional controller with all 18 district accountants reporting directly to her. She would have control and salary review over Meredith in addition to John Grey, the district manager. At the time of annual review, both would consult on the amount of a raise and the performance grading with final salary increases for district accountants being within the guidelines for the division. Also, Meredith would be instructed to follow the directives of both bosses even though those directives might be in conflict with one another from an operational to accounting viewpoint.

In October, John Grey issued the following memo to all employees:

Date: October 23, 1981

TO: All Employees
FROM: John Grey
SUBJECT: Terminations, Suspensions Without Pay, and Grievances

It has come to my attention that there has been some confusion regarding terminations. Let me clarify this by saying that I am the only person who can fire or hire anyone in this district. All suspensions without pay and all employee grievances will be handled by me.

Should you have any questions, please feel free to ask.

This memo reiterated the previous district policy that all hirings and firings would only be carried out by John himself and that all suspensions must be directed by himself and not the supervisors. This memo pleased the hourly and office personnel because although John was admired for his technical knowledge, he was known as a soft touch who would empathize with a sad story. The memo itself did damage to the supervisors, including Meredith, because it negated their power and respect in the eyes of the personnel they supervised and in the eyes of other employees in different departments. Although the work performance continued to remain high in all departments, positive attitudes began to decay, and intergroup conflict was increased.

When conflicts arose among the service group, the sales group, and the accounting staff, John would listen calmly to both sides. Afterwards, although he usually would take no positive action for change, he would explain that "although B. J. shouts a lot, that's just his nature," or "although Dora forgot to give you a message, I'm sure she had a good reason." Finally, after numerous shouting matches among employees when certain situations didn't change, all the supervisors got together informally and decided that any problems among employees would be handled by the supervisors of the departments involved by direct communication.

When Rosa brought B. J. Darling's expense report to the attention of Meredith, Meredith was amazed to find $276 of the required backup receipts and vouchers without dates, company names, or proper explanation of the nature of the expense. Rosa told Meredith that when she had been in the salesmen's office a few hours earlier, she had seen B. J. tearing off the tops of receipts and throwing them in the waste basket. Meredith realized that John had approved the expense report without reviewing the receipts, and since tensions were running high among the departments, she should circumvent the sales manager and go directly to John. After explaining to John that these receipts were unacceptable by the standards created by the home office, John said that he was sure that B. J. had a good reason for doing what he did, but that he would straighten the matter out. Subsequently, when B. J. found his expense report on his desk with a note from John to see him, he stormed into the accounting office, shouting obscenities and accusing Meredith of being out to get him. "You don't have to go out on the road and make money; part of my hard work pays your salary," he shouted. "John had already signed my expense report; you had no right to interfere. . . I can't ever turn my back that somebody isn't trying to stab me." At this point, Meredith had had her fill of all the conflict and simply picked up her car keys and walked out the door.

QUESTIONS

1. Does Meredith seem to be justified in her final reaction? What are some of the stressors that have affected Meredith in her efforts to be a successful manager?
2. What are some of the courses of action open to Meredith, John Grey, or any other employee to reduce the stress caused by the intergroup conflicts?

4

DEBIT, INCORPORATED

Debit, Incorporated was one of the largest public accounting firms in the world. It had offices in virtually every major city, providing auditing, management consulting, and tax services to a wide variety of clientele. As a service company, its major asset was its employees, and it prided itself on the quality of its personnel. Debit hired only the best in the accounting field.

Most of Debit's employees on the auditing staff were recruited at major colleges and universities across the country. Debit extended job offers only to the top accounting students. Most of those offers were accepted because of the students' desire to be affiliated with such a prestigious accounting firm coupled with a most attractive starting salary. To a young graduate, a job offer from Debit was like a ticket to success.

The success ladder at Debit was a short one. In as little as 10 years one could become a partner in the firm. Very few companies could boast of such a short rise to success. Moreover, partners in Debit were highly regarded in the business world. Most graduates found the prospect of reaching the peak of their career before age 35 quite attractive. Nevertheless, making it to partner involved extremely long workweeks, sometimes excessive travel, and 10 long years of total commitment to the firm. As a result, very few employees stayed with Debit long enough to make it to partner. History had shown, however, that as long as you gave it your best, eventually you made it all the way. Although it was not always pleasant working for Debit, there was an unspoken rule that employees had two choices: to quit or to make partner. If one didn't quit, Debit took care of you.

WORK ENVIRONMENT

Debit never pretended to offer a pleasant work environment. Although the compensation was well above that of other firms, Debit got its money's worth out of its employees. It expected each employee to consider the job more important than anything else. This was the reason for the high divorce rate and many family problems among Debit's employees. In essence, each employee was on call seven days a week. Quite often an employee would be told on Friday night that he was to count an inventory out of town on Saturday and Sunday. The fact that he had tickets to the football game of the year or plans for a family reunion did not matter to Debit. In fact, management had created such a cold atmosphere that it would be intimidating for an employee to mention how he had been inconvenienced. Debit held the philosophy that its employees were professionals, and when a job needed to be done, it was their duty to handle it even if the job did not require a professional (for example, driving a partner to the airport).

Debit required that each employee had to turn in a time sheet every two weeks that detailed how every hour had been spent. Hours spent doing work for a client were considered chargeable hours because the time would be billed to the client. The more chargeable hours an employee had, the higher his "utilization" rate would be. Even though an employee had virtually no control over his chargeable hours, he was expected to have a high utilization rate. For those employees who had to spend time driving partners around, the only way to make up for those nonchargeable hours was to work overtime.

Unlike some other accounting firms, Debit did not pay for overtime. It considered its high salaries to be adequate to compensate its employees for any overtime worked. And its employees did work quite a bit of overtime, especially during the busy season, which ran from late November until early April. During that time a typical workweek was somewhere between 50 to 70 hours long. A young staff person once remarked that he had worked so many hours in one year that, on an hourly basis, he was barely earning minimum wage.

EMPLOYEE PERFORMANCE REVIEWS

Since most work had to be performed at the clients' offices, Debit's employees seldom worked in their own office. Even though the professional staff only totaled 70 persons, it sometimes took as long as a year to meet everyone in the company. Employees were assigned to individual clients in task forces. These varied in size depending upon the size of the engagement. Due to the job pressures and the long work hours, these were usually very cohesive groups. The old cliché "misery loves company" best describes the nature of their cohesiveness, particularly for those out-of-town engagements that sometimes lasted for several months. Yet working in small groups for concentrated periods of time gave the person in charge of the engagement a good opportunity to observe the work of his subordinates firsthand. Debit was aware of this management advantage and therefore required the accountants in charge to complete rating reports on each subordinate on an engagement.

The rating reports were the foundation of Debit's performance review process. The rating reports were divided into four major areas: (1) technical; (2) administrative and supervisory; (3) client relations and development; and (4) personal and professional. Within these four areas were statements relating to specific tasks and abilities. For all applicable statements, the reviewer had to rate the subordinate's performance as (1) less than expected; (2) expected; and (3) better than expected. The overall performance in each of the four major areas was then summarized, based on the responses to the related statements. In addition, space was available for supplemental written comments on each major area.

A review session was the discussion of the rating report between the reviewer and the subordinate. When a rating report was due, a reviewer had to complete the form for the subordinate. In addition, the subordinate completed a rating report form as a self-review. The two employees then compared and discussed the two forms. Each of these forms had to be signed by both parties. They were then sent up the ranks to each superior on the engagement until they reached the partner. The forms, as a pair, finally became part of the subordinate's permanent personnel file.

Signing a rating report that your superior prepared for you signified that you read and agreed with the ratings and the comments on the form. Originally, the intent was to make sure that both parties were in agreement and that no incriminating comments reached the personnel file unless they had been seen and understood by the employee. If an employee received a rating or comment that was felt to be unjust, he or she had the opportunity to discuss the problem with the reviewer and try to get it changed. If the reviewer would not change the rating, the employee's only recourse was to bring it to the attention of the reviewer's supervisor.

Rating reports were required for each employee who worked for 80 or more hours on an assignment. On occasion, an employee was assigned to numerous continuous engagements that lasted less than 80 hours. In such instances, it was the responsibility of the employee to periodically request a review. In any case, two reviews were required per quarter for each employee. Debit strictly enforced this rule. As a result, numerous reviews were performed as late as three months after the engagement, often by telephone or hurriedly on weekends. With everyone working long hours or traveling, everyone's goal at quarter-end relating to rating reports was quantity, with little or no regard to quality.

The reason for the need for eight rating reports per person per year was the final step in the performance review process. Since Debit primarily hired recent college graduates, each summer a new group began work. The career paths of the employees within a group were virtually identical. Occasionally, there was a superstar who received an early promotion, but generally there was a basic timeframe for advancement. Debit used these rating reports, along with some grapevine information, in order to rank the individuals within each annual group. Since salaries and promotions were reviewed on an annual basis, this annual ranking helped to determine compensation.

Most annual groups were quite cohesive as a shield against the problems and pressures of such a work environment. Most individuals within a given group also had a good idea where they stood in relation to their peers. The grapevine (Debit had an exceptionally active one) usually found out who was the best in a group and who was the worst. Most everyone else fell in the middle and could not be easily differentiated.

The current class was no different from any previous group. Everyone knew that Charles Thomas was the best of the 15 in the class. He passed the CPA examination on the first try with very high grades. He was doing very well on the job, had a good utilization rate, and some rating reports well worth bragging about. Everyone also knew that Ned Loomis was at the bottom of the totem pole. He did not even take the CPA examination. He lacked technical competence and had a very poor attitude. Nevertheless, neither of these were considered extreme cases. So, as annual review time approached, everyone anticipated that the class would get the blanket promotion, with compensation commensurate to past performance.

Mark Adams was in the current class and he, too, had been comparing himself to his peers and had determined that he was on the upper end of the mid-range. He had interned with Debit during college, passed two parts of the CPA examination, had an adequate utilization rate, and was well liked by everyone. His rating reports had been rather good. He did get two "less than expected" ratings the time he worked for Howard Greene, who expected nothing less than perfection, but he had also accumulated almost a dozen "better than expected" ratings over the course of the year.

At four o'clock one Thursday afternoon, about one week before annual reviews began, Dave Sanger, the partner in charge of personnel, called Mark into his office. Dave handed Mark an envelope and said, "Mark, it seems that we have too many people on our accounting staff. We took a close look at the individuals in your group and found that you have the lowest performance. Here is one month's severance pay."

QUESTIONS

1. While performance reviews are utilized for both planning and control purposes, they often produce dysfunctional consequences. What prob-

lems would you expect from Debit's performance reviews?

2. Why was Mark Adams dismissed? How should
   management have handled this particular situation? As it stands, what will be the impact of
   Mark's dismissal on the rest of the staff?

5

UNIFIED CORPORATION OF AMERICA: ANALYTICAL SERVICES DEPARTMENT

Ken Billingsley, an analytical chemist for the Unified Corporation of America (UCA), sat at his desk staring aimlessly into space. Uncharacteristically, he said nothing as his coworkers walked out of the office and headed home for the evening. During the day, Ken had been in two meetings with his supervisor, Jim Nelson. At the second meeting with Jim, Ken was told that his services at the fibers and plastics division of UCA would no longer be required and he would receive severance pay equivalent to one month's salary. Jim explained that the company was satisfied with Ken's performance of assigned duties, but he had consistently shown an inability to fit in with the group of chemists working in the department. This had led to intragroup problems and poor relations between Ken and his subordinates. The decision to dismiss Ken was made and implemented just 75 days after he had entered the plant as a new employee.

THE COMPANY

UCA was formed in 1920 through the unification of five independent chemically based operations. Throughout the years, the structure of the organization has changed to complement the acquisitions and discharging of production facilities and products. Presently the corporation consists of five distinct divisions: chemicals, fibers and plastics, oil and gas, electrical and electronics, and health and science. Each division is headed by a division president who reports to the chairman of the board.

The Stonewall Plant, located in South Carolina, is the largest plant in the fibers and plastics division. The Stonewall Plant is one of the oldest in the corporation, dating back to the early 1920s when its primary products were agricultural chemicals. Over the years the operations of the plant have changed to accommodate the necessary products of the corporation. The primary product of the plant is an intermediate chemical used in the production of nylon. The process for the manufacturing of this chemical was started in 1951 and has remained the primary product of the plant since that time. Despite the changes in production at the plant, the hourly staffs have remained constant. Most departments throughout the plant have an average seniority of 17 years service to the corporation. It is frequently stated that this long-term service is due to the good benefits negotiated by the union and not to loyalty of the personnel to the company.

THE ANALYTICAL SERVICES DEPARTMENT

Within any manufacturing facility, there is a need for the evaluation of the quality of product produced. The Stonewall Plant has a quality control department consisting of 11 salaried persons and 65 hourly persons. The department has the responsibility of ensuring product quality, giving technical assistance to production, and monitoring plant waste.

The analytical services department is headed by a lab manager who reports directly to the plant manager. Three lab supervisors and a lab foreman report to the lab manager. Each lab supervisor has one to three chemists reporting to him. The lab foreman is in charge of all hourly personnel assigned to the lab and has four chief shift technicians reporting to him. Each chemist has up to eight hourly technicians, known as nonroutine technicians, reporting directly to him/her. These technicians work the day shift only. They have a minimum of 20 years with the company and have arrived at this preferred position primarily through seniority. All other lab technicians, known as routine technicians, work on one of four weekly rotating shifts. Although these people report directly to a chief shift technician, they are subject to the requests of any salaried personnel in the department. The organizational chart for the analytical services department is shown in Figure 5.1.

A chemist in the analytical services department is considered to be a first-line supervisor and has several formal responsibilities. Each person has a specific area of plant operations assigned to him or her and is to give assistance to production personnel to maintain the smooth operations of that area. The maintenance of analytical instrumentation and chemical procedures

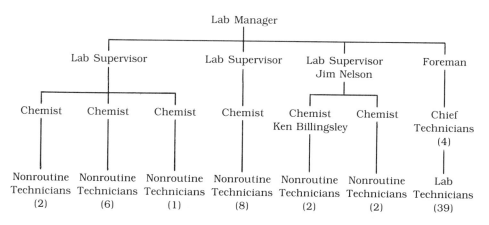

FIGURE 5.1   Analytical services department organizational chart

required to determine the quality of a product is also a responsibility of the chemist. Also, specific projects related to the operations of the delegated production area are assigned to each chemist. The majority of the work is performed by the chemist at a desk where he or she is expected to formulate, initiate, evaluate, and summarize the information generated for a specific project. Most of the actual benchwork is performed by the non-routine technicians assigned to the chemist. All chemists assigned to the department work out of one large office and usually work closely as a group, assisting each other in solving problems and lending the services of their hourly personnel to one another when extra staffing is required.

Under these circumstances, management requires three qualities from their chemists. First, a fundamental knowledge of chemical and instrumental principles necessary for the understanding of plant and lab operations. Second, the ability to work together within a group of peers that have come together from distinctly different backgrounds, who range in age from 24 to 62 years of age, and in years of service from 1 to 40 years. Third, the ability to supervise effectively employees who have worked in the plant for many years and in many instances are unwilling to accept change in their daily routine. When working with these people the chemist must know when to listen to their suggestions and, when the need arises, to invoke change diplomatically.

THE NEW CHEMIST

Ken Billingsley joined UCA in September. He had left the Texas plant of a major chemical company where he also held a chemist position. The move was a lateral

one, but UCA offered Ken more money primarily because he had received a master's degree in chemistry
while maintaining full-time employment. Acquiring
the advanced degree, however, had gained him little or
no rewards from his previous employer.

After contacting some employment agencies, Ken
received the opportunity to interview for a position at
the Stonewall Plant of UCA. The six-hour selection procedure consisted of interviews with a personnel manager, the analytical services department manager, and
two lab supervisors. The four interviewers met at the
end of the day and discussed Ken's potential.

Personnel Manager: Ken's credentials look pretty
    good. He appears to have the qualifications for the
    job. He seemed a little high strung but that may
    have just been nerves.

Lab Supervisor, Lance Nowell: Yes, he seemed to be
    real nervous when I talked to him. When I asked
    him a question he would ramble on and wander to
    many tangential subjects. But overall his position
    in Texas appears to be very similar. He probably
    can do the job.

Lab Supervisor, Jim Nelson: Yes, I believe he can fill
    the position. He seems very well qualified, and
    when he becomes familiar with our organization
    he will settle down.

Lab Manager: I don't know. He may be too high
    strung for this department. He seemed to know
    everything about everything! I have some bad feel-
    ings about his ability to fit in.

Jim Nelson: I think he'll be all right. Anyway, look at
    his credentials. Three years with the company in
    Texas with a master's degree. That would give us
    two chemists with advanced degrees in this de-

partment. It sure will make us look good. I feel once he settles down, he will fit right in.

Lab Manager: Well, Jim, he will be working for you. If you think he can make it then I'll go along. If no one has any objections then we will offer him the position in the next several days.

Ken accepted the position, resigned from his current employer, and moved from Texas to South Carolina.

After the usual paperwork required by the personnel department, Ken was taken to the chemists' office to meet his coworkers. Ken seemed to be a little nervous and appeared to want to become part of the group by continuously adding comments to the conversation. Most of the chemists listened to what Ken said and tried to make him feel comfortable. The group went to lunch together, where Ken constantly interrupted conversations, giving his own opinions and telling of his own experiences. This type of activity went on throughout the day. Two of the chemists, Don and Bill, were walking out of the plant discussing the new man.

Don: I hadn't heard a thing about this guy until today. I had no prejudgements about his personality, but he seems to be a real jerk! You know, I didn't make one comment or tell of one experience that he didn't interrupt me and say how he had done it better or he knew all about it.

Bill: Yes, he does try to give the impression that he knows everything about everything. But he may just be trying to impress us. He'll probably settle down in the next few days.

Don: He'd better! If he tries to supervise those non-routine technicians with that attitude he'll never get anything out of them. Those guys really resent that type of attitude, especially from a new guy.

During the second week of employment, Ken was given the traditional four-day orientation tour of the plant. This tour is somewhat extensive, allowing new salaried employees to meet all department managers, area superintendents, and production supervisors. Usually the orientation group consists of four new employees. At the end of this second week, Jim received several phone calls from the area superintendents and supervisors. The comments made were: "Where did you dig up this new chemist? He is the most obnoxious man I've ever met. He was totally disruptive to the entire orientation group. Who hired him?" These comments bothered Jim for several reasons. This attitude of production personnel toward the lab chemists might strain the working relations between production and the lab. Also, the question "Who hired him?" kept coming up. Jim knew that this was putting him in a bad position. Everyone who asked the question knew who had made the decision.

Ken received his first project assignment during his third week. The second day after this assignment, Ken asked to meet with Jim and the following exchange took place:

Ken: Jim, you know I can do more work than this project requires. This will only take a few hours a day for the next several weeks to complete. In my previous job, I had three or four projects constantly assigned to me. I want more work.

Jim: Ken, we like to take things slow with a new man. As you put more time in with us we will expect more out of you. Just do your best on this project and then we'll get more for you to do. Also, I need to talk to you about your attitude. I've heard a lot of comments about the statement, "When I was in Texas. . . ." Here at UCA we have our own way of doing things. People don't like to be constantly criticized about the way they perform their jobs. This applies to the other chemists as well as the technicians. I'm sure that as you become accustomed to the ways we do things here, you'll fit right into our system.

Ken's attitude and personality did not change during the next several weeks. He was constantly being laughed at behind his back by chemists, technicians, and by Jim. Most of Ken's coworkers tried to avoid him, and none of the lab chemists associated with him outside of the office. Some of the chemists tried talking to Ken about his attitudes, but came away feeling like they had achieved nothing. The technicians working for Ken did what they were told, but there was the constant realization that they had no respect for the man. Some of the chemists openly commented that this lack of respect for one chemist might spill over to their people if they were not careful.

On the morning of December 10th, Jim had the last of several meetings with Ken about his personality. When the meeting was over, Jim felt this one was as worthless as the previous sessions had been about initiating a change. Later that morning Jim met with the lab manager and resigned himself to the fact that Ken did not have any future with UCA. Jim called Ken into his office during the early afternoon.

Jim: Ken, as you know by our previous conversations, there have been some problems between you and the other chemists, as well as the technicians. Although your work has been satisfactory, it is our decision to terminate your employment effective immediately. You will receive one month's salary as severance pay. I'm sorry things didn't work out. You just haven't fit into our system. Elmer (the lab manager) said he would see you if you wanted to talk to him about this.

Ken: I can't believe this! I had no idea this was even being contemplated. I left a good job to come here. In three years there I didn't have any problems. And I just closed on a house. I don't know what to say.

Jim: I'm sorry, but this decision is final. The personnel manager will see you this afternoon. I suggest that you wait until after the other chemists leave before cleaning out your desk.

QUESTIONS

1. What are the group conflicts implied in the case that prompted the lab manager and Jim to terminate Ken's employment?

2. How could Jim have handled the situation between Ken and the other department members more proficiently?

3. What effect would Ken's dismissal have on the other department members in the future?

6

ANDERSON CLOTHING, INC.

The Anderson Company is one of the largest manufacturers of exclusive men's wear in the eastern United States. The company has experienced a pattern of continued growth since it was organized in 1950. Approximately 85 stores specializing in men's clothing are served by the Anderson Company.

After significant increases in sales volume and profitability during the 1950s and early 1960s, the company decided to begin data processing operations within the company rather than continuing with the use of a service bureau's facilities. Subsequently a data processing department was created at Anderson in 1967, and seven people were hired to organize the department and begin its operations. By 1969 the complexity of the expanding data processing operations necessitated the hiring of a full-time technical analyst to provide expertise in various areas of operations.

David Fisher, a technical analyst with four years previous experience as a highly skilled technician, was hired to fill this position at a salary level above the average for the industry. David was 25 years old, single, a high school graduate, and had attended college for approximately two-and-a-half years. All of the psychological and aptitude tests administered by the company during the interviewing process indicated that he was well suited for the position—alert, well organized, highly motivated, and technically skilled. He had a warm, friendly personality and displayed an energetic style without being overly aggressive.

DAVID: THE TECHNICIAN

During the first three years of his employment David was the sole technical analyst for the company's data processing department. During this time he was seemingly highly motivated, and this motivation extended not only to his assigned duties but also to other projects. His assigned duties required him to find solutions to complex problems and situations encountered by others that they could not resolve. He was also responsible for developing and teaching technical classes and seminars. In addition to these assigned responsibilities, he developed computer products that he felt could be used for enhancing the operations of the company's data processing department. Because of their marketability these products were later sold to other companies. All of these tasks were accomplished at the above-average or outstanding level.

The data processing staff at Anderson highly respected David for his technical and problem-solving abilities and his ability to communicate technical jargon in terms that they could understand. From time to time he would receive praise and recognition from his peers because of his performance, and salary increases and promotions from his manager.

DAVID: THE MANAGER

By 1972 the data processing staff had expanded to 35 individuals. This growth required the technical support staff to expand in order to support the increased demand for technical services. In light of this need, two individuals from the nontechnical area who were interested in the technical field were promoted to the level of junior technical analysts. This action was accompanied by David's promotion to manager of technical analysts.

To some degree David was pleased with this most recent promotion. However, he also had some misgivings about his ability to be effective in this position. In particular (a) he had had no prior training or experience in the area of management and (b) he was aware that company policy required that a manager spend a minimum of 75 percent of his time in administrative duties and the remaining time performing other functions. David's special affinity for technical duties and the uncertainty about administrative functions caused him to experience a good deal of anxiety. However, he assumed the new responsibilities.

The transition from technician to manager was difficult for David. He just could not become enthusiastic about pushing paper and listening to people problems. His effectiveness and efficiency for getting his tasks accomplished began to diminish. David also felt less desire to be innovative or to "make things happen" but rather he was contented to do just what was absolutely required and no more.

Although David realized that at this point in his career he was not happy in his role as a manager, he also believed that there currently was no other position available for him to assume at Anderson. As such he decided just to make the best of things until either (1) he developed an interest in managerial activities, (2) a more favorable opportunity arose, or (3) he decided to leave the company. He was delaying option (3) as long as possible because the company had an excellent working environment and had compensated him well for his services. Neither David nor his manager felt very comfortable talking to each other about the problem and consequently avoided discussing it as much as possible. In the meantime, David continued to receive above average performance evaluations and salary increases.

DAVID: THE PROJECT LEADER

Approximately three years after David's promotion to manager of technical analysts, the data processing department made a decision to upgrade its operations significantly. This developmental project would require the effort of a team of six people working full-time for approximately one-and-a-half to two years. This team would be comprised of two technical persons and four nontechnical persons. Finding four nontechnical individuals to join the team was a relatively easy task. However, filling the technical positions presented a different problem. Because of the level of expertise needed for the technical side of the project, management's first inclination was to hire persons from outside the company who had the required experience. However, remembering their strong feelings about David's technical abilities and aptitude, they offered to train him for one of the two positions. After the training period he would assume the duties of co-project leader for the technical activities of the project. This position would be primarily a hands-on opportunity with light administrative duties rather than one that was predominantly administrative. This opportunity appealed to David and he accepted the offer.

Throughout the duration of this project David showed vital signs of increased enthusiasm, interest, and effectiveness. He also began using his creative abilities again in various areas of the project's development.

While working on this project, the team was physically separated from the remainder of the data processing personnel so that they would not be interrupted with the day-to-day problems and activities of the department. Although this arrangement did serve its intended purpose, there was also an associated disadvantage. Various changes were occurring within the mainstream of the department's operations relative to the direction in which the data processing department was headed. These changes were precipitated primarily from the needs of the organization as well as other technological advances in automation. Unfortunately very little information concerning these changes filtered to these team members because of their isolation. These changes in organization needs and data processing needs would certainly affect the team members at project completion.

DAVID: THE FRUSTRATED TECHNICIAN

Upon completion of this project in 1977 David and other members of the team had to be diffused back into the mainstream of day-to-day activities. For some members of the team this was not so difficult. For others, including David, it presented a more difficult endeavor. The position that David had held before joining the development team had been assumed by another individual. The need for a technical "guru" had been replaced with the need for a different type of technical "guru" due to the changes in organizational and departmental direction.

Faced with this problem, management decided to create a position for David within the technical area, letting him design the job functions according to his skills and interests and the needs of the department. This process of job definition proved to be very difficult and frustrating for David. He didn't know what the needs of the department were—and frankly, he was not quite sure that management knew inasmuch as they had not communicated these needs to him.

At this point David felt that he was being side-tracked and that there was little left to do except begin looking for employment elsewhere. But because of his high salary level at Anderson and his lack of a college degree, David believed that it would be extremely difficult to find another job without taking a sizable reduction in salary—and he had adjusted his lifestyle to his current financial level. As a consequence he decided to delay searching for another job and to begin working toward his bachelor's degree in order to overcome his barrier. Furthermore, his lack of significant responsibilities at Anderson would give him time to study at the office. After beginning his courses, he found that studying presented a challenge that partially filled the void left by his employment.

For two years David's manager, Tom Winston, allowed this condition to exist until finally he decided that in the best interest of the organization, David, and himself, this issue must be addressed and dealt with, as difficult as it might be. On the performance evaluation report that followed, Tom made the following comments:

> David Fisher, in my opinion, is one of the most skilled and experienced members of the Anderson Company's staff. His communication skills are excellent—both written and verbal. His job knowledge extends from extensive general concepts to the very technical. Many people with these skills (or traits) tend to be loners, but this is not the case with David.

In preparing David's review, however, I would be very remiss if I didn't express my deep concern over the effectiveness of David's role at Anderson and the value of service that Anderson receives. Simply stated, his effectiveness and productivity is much below the level it should be for a person of his skill and experience. This is bad from both a personal and company standpoint. It is very evident that he is indeed frustrated with his overall role, effectiveness, and responsibilities.

The real issue of David's review is why we have a highly skilled technical individual who is underutilized, who is not as effective as he should be, and has not provided the level of productivity the company should expect.

Placing the blame for this situation is complicated by the individual's actions, management's actions, and the organization environment.

Because of the sensitive nature of this matter, Tom Winston invited the department's director, with David's approval, to enter a round of discussions in an effort to resolve the situation. During these discussions David made the following statements concerning his feeling about his role at Anderson:

I had a feeling of being needed through the end of the development project. After that I felt as though the company was trying to create something just to accommodate me. I have not beforehand expressed my real feelings because I am not the most aggressive person by nature—and after a time I wasn't sure that anybody cared about what I had to say.

Most recently I see myself as being the fifth wheel in the department. I have not been pleased with my responsibilities or performance over the past couple years and I've just kept hoping things would change, but it just goes on and on.

QUESTIONS

1. What are the primary reasons for the apparent difference in David's motivation levels during his roles as technician and manager? What role did financial rewards play in motivating David?

2. What could management do to lessen David's frustration and enhance his motivation during the transition from technician to manager?

3. What issues should be addressed by the two managers and David during their rounds of discussion so that some decision(s) could be made regarding the effective utilization of David in the future?

7

EMERALD FINANCIAL CORPORATION

Emerald Financial Corporation was founded in 1932 to provide financing for its parent company, a major industrial firm producing a widely diversified array of products for home, industry, and government. Emerald Financial Corporation has grown since 1932 from a small company with limited markets into one of the nation's largest financial service firms. The firm finances a wide range of items including chemical plants, mobile homes, aircraft, construction equipment, furniture, and computers.

CONSUMER FINANCING DEPARTMENT

Bill Joyner is the area manager of Emerald and is responsible for a consumer financing department. He is 26 years old, married, has one child, and is a graduate in economics from State University. Although Bill has been area manager for only three months, he has three years service with Emerald and has served as branch manager in another office.

Bill's department primarily offers direct cash loans, usually secured by second mortgages. In addition, the office finances home improvement and lends to other consumer finance companies. The office has only been marginally productive in recent months and has experienced increasing problems. The condition of the economy, with rising unemployment and a depressed housing market, has had negative effects on the performance of the office. Performance has also been affected by increased absenteeism and turnover including the unexpected firing of the office manager and Bill Joyner's subsequent arrival.

Due to his predecessor's quick dismissal, there has been no real adjustment period for Bill in his new environment. He has been thrust into managing the daily activities of an unfamiliar office, staffed with employees unknown to him. The only real input and guiding force he has to assist him is his district manager, Mary Evans, whose office is 100 miles away.

Bill has 10 subordinates, including a 25-year-old credit manager whom he worked with when they both began with the company, and a 36-year-old collection manager with over 10 years experience in the finance industry. In addition, he has five management trainees in various stages of the company's Management Development Program. They are all college graduates and range in age from 22 to 30. The balance of his office includes a 30-year-old senior clerk, a 28-year-old collection expeditor, and a 21-year-old clerk/computer operator.

The level of conflict within the office is not detrimental. When conflicts arise, the solution to them is usually beneficial to the office operations and results in improved conditions. There are no recognizable groups within the office, though a few of the employees are good friends and see each other socially. The majority of the employees see each other socially only on rare special occasions.

THE LEADERSHIP OF BILL JOYNER

Bill Joyner might be described as a job-centered leader rather than an employee-centered one. Three months ago, when Bill arrived, he held a short meeting to introduce himself and give some very general views on managing the office. He indicated no major changes in daily activities. He then met individually with each employee, and together they reviewed the employee's goals and objectives and the company's expectations. Goal setting was completed in a very general sense. Bill also stressed to everyone that he would always be available if anyone had questions, problems, or suggestions.

Since his arrival, Bill has often been approached by his employees over various concerns. His management trainees are especially frequent visitors to his office, or are overheard by him in conversations among themselves. It seems that they are often bored and frustrated because they don't have enough work to occupy a full day. Yet they are required to work late hours, often two nights per week, and frequently on Saturdays. These hours have been necessary in order to contact customers who work during the day. When the trainees have idle time, they are not allowed to work on their management development program by reviewing company instructions and policies that they are expected to be familiar with in order to complete their programs. Bill has indicated each time he is approached that changes are in order and that some corrective action will be taken. So far, everything remains the same.

Bill Joyner is presently more concerned with performance than with his employees' satisfaction. His immediate concern, however, is an employee, Keith Roberts, who has been with Emerald for approximately 18 months as a management trainee. He is 23 years old, and this represents his first job since graduating with a business degree from a local university.

Recently, Keith seems to be spending more and more time away from his desk. He has missed many hours of work due to car trouble, illness, and dentist appointments. When he is at work and at his desk, he sits idly much of the time, or discusses subjects other than business with his coworkers. Yet his work is still completed each day, and its quality has not been visibly affected.

Bill has been noticeably concerned about what he views as Keith's poor attitude. He has spent more and more time on the phone in hushed conversations with his district manager. However, he has had no private conversations with Keith. He has only generally mentioned the problems to the entire group during office meetings.

Last Tuesday, Keith didn't go to work at all, nor did he phone the office. His explanation on Wednesday when he returned was that he had had car trouble and had spent the entire day in the shop. Things were obviously tense, yet Bill still did not speak with Keith. Finally, on Friday about thirty minutes prior to closing, Bill called Keith into his office. About 20 minutes later, Keith emerged. He grabbed his briefcase and a few loose items, and left the office. Few people noticed.

Bill entered the outer office about five minutes later and called an office meeting. He made some general announcements, reviewed the weekly report of figures, and asked if there was any discussion or questions. As everyone readied to leave for the weekend, he added quietly, "After today, Keith will no longer be with us. Have a nice weekend."

Everyone walked out of the office in shock. No one spoke until they reached the parking lot, but there they began to discuss what had just happened. They talked about how Keith was so well liked and intelligent. They remembered the many times he had provided a laugh when things were going badly. They believed he had been fired with no warning. No attempt had been made by management to discuss Keith's situation with him and to identify the problem underlying his deteriorating work situation. To *their* knowledge, Keith had been given no indication that his performance was any less than satisfactory.

On Monday following Keith's dismissal, the remaining employees are still confused and concerned about Friday's events. They are afraid that their performances might also be termed unsatisfactory—without their being aware of it. They are afraid to ask the details of Keith's dismissal, and their fears linger and grow. They are afraid to make decisions for fear of making a critical mistake. They are even afraid when performing their normal tasks, fearing they will unknowingly do the wrong thing. Everyone appears to be working diligently—no coffee breaks, no personal phone calls, no conversations unrelated to business. Work is completed as usual by day's end, but no one feels good about it and the tension is almost unbearable. Performance doesn't appear to be measurably lessened, but this new attitude doesn't improve performance either. Morale is obviously low.

Now, Bill Joyner realizes that though he has rid himself of what he perceived as his most pressing problem—Keith—he may have created a larger one. He must improve his office's performance by reporting improved and more consistent figures each month. He faces, however, a group of employees whom he hardly knows. A group that has never seemed to be happy or satisfied with their jobs and who now also appear to mistrust the new boss.

Bill realizes that he must take some action, but he is uncertain of what he should do. He dials the number of his district manager, closes his office door, and once again asks her advice on what action he should take.

QUESTIONS

1. Do you believe that a change in Bill Joyner's leadership style might be appropriate for this situation?

2. What difficulties might be encountered if he does attempt to change his style of leadership?

3. What can Bill do to increase employee motivation and satisfaction in his department?

8

CUSTOM AUDIO, INC.

Claire Johnson had just finished another meeting with her immediate supervisor, Bob Clemmons, and his supervisor, Adam Hoefling. They had met to discuss the continuing problems Claire was having with her job as budget director for Custom Audio. Claire left the meeting feeling extremely frustrated—she had wanted to discuss the overall problem and possible solutions, but once in the meeting found that her superiors wanted to talk about one particular area and she was not able to redirect the meeting. Claire realized that she had come to the point where she needed to make a decision on how to handle the problem and implement a solution.

COMPANY BACKGROUND

Custom Audio was founded in 1949 by David Stein as a door-to-door television sales company. Over the years, through his personal perseverance and a keen sense of the television, appliance, and audio markets, David built the company up to be one of the most successful appliance and audio retailers in the country. The company's major growth occurred in the late 1960s and early 1970s as it capitalized on the booming audio business. It opened many outlets throughout the Southeast that catered to college students—a previously untapped market that had the knowledge to select audio equipment from a large selection and had the money to spend on the merchandise. The outlets initially were discount supermarkets for audio equipment.

As the range of audio equipment expanded, and electronics entered the market, the company expanded its product line in order to become an industry leader. During this time, the company also sought to diversify and acquired many different companies, such as gasoline and furniture retailers. The company also acquired a retail company that leased audio and appliance departments in a large West Coast discount retailer.

In 1970, David's son Leonard took over the presidency of Custom Audio. After a severe economic recession in 1975, he continued the growth his father had started, not by diversifying but by expanding existing operations. The outlets previously geared toward college students were updated and expanded to keep up with students as they left school, took jobs, and married. All stores began to carry televisions and microwave ovens, and the supermarket approach was phased out. Until 1980, Custom Audio sold appliances only in its Baltimore store and on the west coast. During 1981 the company expanded its appliance operations into Georgia, where it already had successful audio operations. The west coast division also expanded quite rapidly, adding 12 stores during the year. The majority of the expansion was complete by February, 1982, but it and a worsening economy had placed financial strain on the company.

CLAIRE'S PROMOTION

Claire began to work for Custom Audio in January, 1979, as a staff accountant in the general ledger department. After nine months as a staff accountant, she was promoted to corporate cash manager. A year later

she assumed the additional responsibilities of the corporate insurance program. Her immediate superior
was John Klein, the treasurer, with whom she had developed a good, but not close, relationship. She knew
that she had earned his respect for her work and felt
able to discuss any problems freely with him. Since her
cash and insurance responsibilities required her to
work closely with the general ledger department, she
also developed a good relationship with Bob Clemmons, an assistant controller in the Baltimore office.

In October, 1981, Claire found out that the budget
director was leaving, and she immediately approached
John Klein about the job. She pushed very hard for the
job, as she had wanted it for some time. After two
weeks, and interviews with Leonard Stein and all the
company vice presidents, Claire was offered the job.
When John offered her the job he informed her that she
would not report to him, but would report to Bob. He
explained that the move had been planned for some
time and had nothing to do with her personally. This
caused Claire to have some reservations about taking
the job.

Initially she knew that while working for John, she
had considerable autonomy. While she consulted with
John frequently, she was encouraged to make her own
decisions and use him more for guidance than as a
decision-maker. The accounting department was not
noted for the autonomy granted its managers, or assistant controllers, for that matter. Since the structure
of the budgeting job required autonomy, Claire was
somewhat concerned.

In addition, because the budgeting job came under John's direction, the budget director handled not
only the actual budgeting, but also projects including
the company's financial projections, any financial analysis required, and miscellaneous research projects assigned by Leonard Stein or John Klein. Claire felt that

moving into accounting, she would lose the projects and control over the budgeting function and would become a glorified staff accountant. The projects and the growth they offered were the main reason Claire wanted the job. Finally, Claire felt that a true promotion would have been to an assistant controllership level, and as a result of the change in reporting structure, the job change was only a horizontal move.

Claire discussed these issues with John and he assured her that they posed no problem. The job she was accepting was the same one her predecessors had, and the move was not horizontal because of the increased responsibility. Based on his assurances she accepted the job.

Work began immediately on the budgets for the fiscal year beginning in March, 1982. Also, since the company had found no one to replace her in her old capacity, Claire continued to handle the cash and insurance. Despite the fact that she had one budget clerk and two cash/insurance clerks working for her, and she delegated most of the cash functions to her clerks, Claire found herself working 78-80 hours a week just to keep up the vital functions of both jobs. Despite everyone's efforts, a backlog of work developed because the department was, in effect, one person short.

Claire worked almost exclusively on budgets from December through March. By the end of March, the final budgets had been approved and Claire was preparing to verify and proof the budgets before consolidating the corporate figures for the April board of directors meeting. Instead she had to stop work on the budgets and begin work on the year-end audit. In her cash and insurance capacities Claire was responsible for a number of audit schedules, many of which were due or past due. Claire was so late on the final schedules she had to prepare that there was a real possibility that the entire audit would not be completed on time.

As a result, Bob and Adam Wilson, the controller, pushed her constantly about her work. John Klein had arranged for her to receive some help during the initial audit work, but now when she would ask for help from Bob, it was flatly denied.

Soon afterward John called Claire in for a heart-to-heart talk. During the meeting they spoke of the problems encountered during the budgeting and the audit. By then Claire had realized that her new bosses neither knew nor understood the budgeting process, nor did she feel that they cared. As she and John talked, Claire expressed this and other concerns, such as the problem she was having keeping two jobs up. She stated that she felt that every time she tried to stand up, someone was waiting to knock her down. John appeared to be familiar with her problems and was very receptive to taking action to correct them. Claire left the meeting feeling that her problems would be solved.

A few days after her meeting with John, he told her that he had hired Andrew Lyons as an assistant treasurer, and he would provide some relief within two weeks. Claire assumed that Andrew would replace her as cash and insurance manager.

It became apparent, though, within a week after Andrew came to work for Custom Audio, that he had no intention of handling the work Claire had done. Both Andrew and John continued to funnel cash and insurance work to Claire. When Leonard and John began assigning projects to Claire, Bob and Adam reacted negatively and attempted to take the work from Claire so Bob could handle it. On top of this, Claire was trying to finalize the budgets and clean up the backlog of work that had accumulated since October.

As her frustration grew, Claire made several attempts to talk to John, Adam, and Bob about her situation. She learned, through these attempts, that Andrew was not hired as her replacement but to handle overflow from John's work. Andrew was responsible for the cash and insurance, but he was not expected to do the "pencil pushing" required to do the job. Claire was expected to handle that work until a decision was made on a more systematic approach to that aspect of the job. She also learned that Bob and Adam had a very narrow view of the budgeting function and did not feel she should be receiving projects from Leonard and John.

As Claire learned more about her superiors' impression about her situation, her anger and frustration grew. After this last meeting, she realized that she had been handling two jobs for eight months and there was little relief in sight. She also realized that she was close to the breaking point, and something needed to be done soon. She went back to her office to decide on a course of action.

QUESTIONS

1. What are the key factors operating in the case that prevent Claire from resolving her frustration with the workload she is trying to handle?

2. What steps should Claire take to resolve the problems?

3. As Claire's boss, what steps would you take to relieve the anxiety and frustration?

9

VECTOR ALUMINUM COMPANY

Paul Covington is a senior applications analyst for Corporate Systems in the information systems department at Vector Aluminum Company. He has six years experience in the field and has been promoted rapidly with his previous employers. He came to work for Vector nearly two years ago and has done the same job for the same pay the entire time. He took the job at Vector because of a slightly higher salary but also because he wanted to work in a more challenging corporate environment with greater opportunity to be rewarded for doing good work.

COMPANY BACKGROUND

Vector Aluminum Company produces a number of products ranging from aluminum ingots to precision aluminum machinery components. Vector is in *Fortune's 500* with annual sales of about six billion dollars. They are located in Capital City in a modern plush facility that is considered an architectural showcase in the area. However, the current year has not been kind to Vector. Profits have fallen off 44 percent from last year despite the sale of fixed assets that resulted in a huge one-time exceptional gain. Currently one-third of the factory workers have been laid off and there is a wage freeze in effect for those employees who still have their jobs.

A TEST OF LOYALTY VERSUS PERSONAL SURVIVAL?

Paul Covington sat at his desk and neatly moved computer printouts from one stack to another. His current assignment had been on his desk for nearly three months now. While he had knocked out a lot of other projects during that time, this one was extremely difficult and frustrating.

It was a far cry from last November when Paul had confidently walked into his supervisor's office for his first annual review. On a scale of 1 to 7 Paul had received five "7's," one "6," and one "5." He was recommended for a two-step raise, and he was proud of the effort he had put in and glad to see that it was going to pay off. He couldn't wait to tell his wife he'd be getting nearly $400 extra per month. They were planning to buy a new house, so the money was already earmarked for the new house payment.

Two weeks later Paul's manager, Stoney Coleman, called him and his project teammates into the manager's office and announced, "Because of decreased orders for aluminum, we are going to have to freeze all wages. I don't know how long it will last, but these things have happened in the past and I'm sure that it will be over in a few months at the most." Paul was disappointed, but he was a team player and recognized the situation. He did not intend to look for another job. Instead he changed his tax filing status to bring home more money each check and assumed the raise was coming soon anyway.

Paul was also working on his MBA degree and had to come up with nearly $800 for tuition up front in the fall. Fortunately he and his wife, Debbie, had some money in savings to cover it until Vector reimbursed them for it at the end of the semester. Debbie was a medical assistant, and her salary helped make ends meet in the Covington household.

The wage freeze, of course, was not very popular, and within a month three people had left Vector. Although he saw no actual evidence, Paul heard that they were making half again as much as he. A month later Paul received notice of the annual stockholders meeting (Paul owns several shares through Vector's Employee Savings and Investment Plan). He nearly passed out when he read that Shorty Vector, the founder's grandson, received nearly one and a half million dollars in compensation, and he nearly fell out of his chair when he read that the treasurer got a bonus of $200,000 for exceptional work. Paul began to look at other ways of making money, and started to develop a spare-time business of his own, which began to grow slowly but surely.

Weeks and months passed, and Paul's work at Vector began to suffer. He didn't enjoy his job as much as a year ago and was given an assignment that he regarded as insignificant, boring busywork. He was told to find out why two reports, with a total dollar figure of nearly two million dollars, were out of balance by one cent! A month later, while still searching for the first cent, he was given a similar project: locate a 13¢ difference between total dollars paid to all employees ten weeks ago and what the payroll department now says that it should have been. During this time Paul was also given his usual assortment of projects that he took pride in finishing early and in less time than originally requested. He also took pride in seeing a finished product leave his hand and be passed to a satisfied user department.

After about five months Paul was frustrated and felt that he had been shortchanged by Vector. He saw that the wage freeze was not going to be ending anytime soon. The newspaper's want ad section became daily reading material for Paul, who felt that he had done an exceptional job for the company. Additionally, his spare-time business was requiring more time. It was not yet profitable enough to go into full time, but Paul could see that it would be soon enough, and he preferred to spend his extra time on it. Consequently, he avoided overtime like a plague.

That same month, Debbie was hit by a car and her injuries forced her to quit her job at the doctor's office. Although Debbie's salary had been considered a luxury, it now looked like a necessity. Their savings account was being slowly depleted. That was the case until Paul's car burst into flames while driving to work one day. The resulting engine rebuilding job was estimated at $1,100 and two days later, Debbie's car ground to a halt also, requiring $428 for repairs. The savings account was no longer being slowly depleted, it was nearly gone.

"I'm sick and tired of this and I'm not going to take it any more," Paul felt like shouting from his window. He went to Jane Niles, the personnel manager, and the following conversation took place:

Paul: Jane, I am basically satisfied with my job here at Vector, but I am starting to have some financial difficulties that the wage freeze is contributing strongly to. (Paul then related his recent events to Jane.)

Jane: I know, we're all hurting because of it, but our hands are tied. Until top management like Shorty Vector decide to lift the freeze, there's nothing we can do. Please don't leave, Paul. You're doing really good work and we don't want to lose you.

Paul: As I said, I don't want to leave, but it's fast getting to the point that I'm going to have to. I feel that we have a different situation than most in the department. We have mostly men working here, and they are the primary bread winners in most cases. We can survive without Debbie's full salary, but my salary is food on the table and the house payment. Furthermore, most data processing professionals will have no problem finding a job elsewhere, even in today's depressed economy. You won't just lose me, you'll lose others.

Jane: I know. I wish there were something that we could do about it.

About two weeks later, Paul was given the opportunity to interview with another department for a small pay raise. It was in a different location 45 minutes from Paul's house, through two toll booths, in a shop so small that there would be minimal chance for advancement. Paul felt that the small increase was not worth the additional time and money spent to commute, especially in light of the slim chance of promotion. He turned it down and started to contemplate seriously his future at Vector.

QUESTIONS

1. What is Paul's primary problem at Vector Aluminum?

2. What can Vector Aluminum in general and Stoney Coleman in particular do to resolve Paul's problem?

3. What are Paul's alternative courses of action given his treatment by Vector? What are the advantages/disadvantages to each alternative?

10

LARK, INC.

Lark, Inc., a large international food company, has experienced excellent growth and market share increases over its 50-year history. Begun by a single entrepreneur, Lark has developed, through innovation and acquisition, several leading commodities and products within the food industry. Through the development and effective implementation of extensive marketing programs and strong support by its large sales force, the company has continued to grow and prosper nationwide.

In recent years, however, the level of sales in the southern division of Lark has not kept pace with the sales increases of other divisions despite the tremendous population growth within the division. Although the majority of sales and marketing programs are corporately controlled, divisional managers have the latitude to modify marketing plans and are in complete control of their personnel.

SOUTHERN DIVISION

Ed Cook, 61, division manager for the past eight years, is an extremely dynamic individual who has worked his way up the corporate sales ladder and adapted well to the numerous changes in operations and structures within the company and industry over the past 30 years. He is a forceful individual who likes to maintain a firm control of all aspects of the divisional operations, quite a task for an operation of this size. Although the organizational structure facilitates delegation of authority to the regional managers and product managers, Ed retains full authority, and all decisions other than the most routine are made by Ed. All feedback to Ed is either supportive of his decisions or if not, totally ignored and discouraged.

As a result of Ed's management style, he has surrounded himself with individuals who fit the yes-man role and who actually work in fear of doing anything to displease Ed. Consequently, his staff is reluctant to make any decisions or promote any new ideas or techniques. Therefore, business continues to operate as it has in the past in spite of changes in the environment.

Steve Gant, divisional product manager, exemplifies the individual on Ed Cook's staff. Steve had worked under Ed when Ed was a regional manager and was promoted to product manager a few years after Ed became division manager. A divisional product manager's job entails adaptation and communication of corporate deals and promotions to the individual districts within the division. Due to customer and competitive conditions within the various districts, the corporate plans must be modified at the various district levels. Steve, however, is an extremely nervous individual who easily becomes frustrated when presented with any type of problem requiring a change. Therefore, once his plans have been approved by Ed Cook, Steve is extremely reluctant to approve any type of change requested by district managers to satisfy a need in their district. As a result, unless extreme pressure is applied by the district managers for a change to meet their needs, the plans remain as is, and potential business may be lost.

Another member of Ed Cook's circle is Bob Smith, regional manager. Bob was hired as a sales representative by Ed when Ed was a district manager. Bob has systematically moved up the corporate ladder and remained under the close tutelage of Ed. Although Bob has been recognized as an effective manager, like Ed he can only deal effectively with those who take his word as gospel. His management orientation does not allow him the flexibility of dealing with the newer employees who occasionally ask the question "why?" Bob is considered to be the most successful manager in the division in dealing with Ed Cook. In fact, Ed respects Bob's opinion and ideas and is often receptive to them. However, Bob has adopted Ed's management technique of retaining his power and not delegating responsibility and encourages the same type of puppetry from his district managers as Ed does of his subordinates.

A refreshing variation in management style is exhibited by Elvin Powers. As a result of corporate geographic restructuring, Elvin was transferred from the eastern division to be district manager in the southern division. Elvin is extremely open-minded and encourages suggestions and constructive criticism from his subordinates. He also effectively delegates work responsibility and the authority necessary to carry out the tasks. The cohesive working team under Elvin's direction functioned very efficiently and led the division for four consecutive years. He is extremely effective in coercing product managers and divisional management to implement programs he desires for his market. However, Elvin did not fit in well with the management style of either Ed Cook or Bob Smith although he was often more successful. To alleviate the problem of not being able to "handle" Elvin, he was promoted to regional manager in another division.

Elvin was replaced as district manager with Keith Dodson, an individual having the characteristics Ed prefers in his market managers. Keith is reluctant to make any type of decision regardless of its immediacy. Keith would make no decision but rather say that he would get back to you, which seldom happened. Regardless of the urgency of a situation, he would first check with Bob Smith on even the most minute decision. As a consequence of Keith's leadership (or lack of it), morale and business have tapered off considerably from the level of Elvin's regime. The strengths of the individuals Elvin put together in his sales team are the only things that keep business rolling.

The management climate that is prevalent at the top of the sales structure has also permeated the lower-level, sales supervisory positions. Bill Dunsford, sales supervisor, is an old friend of Ed Cook and has held this position for several years. Although he is responsible for training, directing, and motivating the sales force, Bill is simply "riding out" his last few years before retiring. Bill has failed to stay up on the changing business environment as well as the ever-changing internal procedures. As a result, Bill is a demotivator instead of motivator of his people. Although local management and probably even Ed Cook realize this situation, nothing has been done about it. Bill has given the best years of his life and has performed very well for Lark until the past few years. Since Bill has always been a fine company man, Ed is reluctant to take any steps that would hurt Bill's ego. As a result, the sharp young sales representatives are extremely discontented over their lack of help and support from Bill.

Ned Gravitts, account executive, typifies the young, educated potential managers for Lark. Ned and his counterparts effectively implement the marketing and sales programs despite the ineffective management of people like Bill and Keith. Sales representatives under Bill communicate directly with Ned, who attempts to provide them with the direction and motivation needed, since Bill Dunsford has neglected to do so. Consequently, Ned is actually assuming the responsibility for his own job as account executive, Bill's as supervisor, and part of Keith's as market manager.

PREPARATION FOR A SUCCESSOR

As a result of Ed Cook's practice of maintaining tight, personal control over any substantive decisions, the issue of selecting his successor has considerable implications for Lark in general and the southern division in particular. Although he has experienced a degree of success, Ed is nearing retirement and has not adequately developed any successors for either himself or the regional or district managers in his age group.

Of a more specific concern, at the lower levels of the division, is the issue of potential leaders like Ned Gravitts being "run off" due to lack of opportunity and frustration with the operation of the organization and incompetence of many of its managers. With the supervisory positions being tied up with individuals like Bill, there is no room for advancement, and after several years as account executive, people like Ned are looking to other companies for future opportunities. Also, considering the promotion of individuals like Steve Gant and Keith Dodson, people like Ned realize that they do not fit into the mold of the type of individuals this division appears to be looking for as its future management.

Even at the field sales level, when managers like Keith and supervisors like Bill accidently hire someone with management potential, they also become frustrated with the misdirected supervision from individuals such as Bill Dunsford and the lack of advancement opportunities resulting from slots being tied up with people like Bill.

Ed Cook has finally begun to realize the critical leadership shortage he has created within his division. However, confronted with the fact that the management team he is working with includes all his personal friends and that he only has three years until retirement, Ed is totally perplexed as to the steps he should take to rectify the situation.

QUESTIONS

1. What immediate action should Ed Cook take to rectify his management team crisis?

2. What actions should Lark's headquarters take to turn the sales picture around in the southern division?

3. What should be done with managers such as Keith Dodson and Steve Gant?

11

SOUTHERN LEASING COMPANY, INC.

The accounting staff of the Southern Leasing Company suddenly found themselves without a manager. Their previous manager, Thomas Johnson, had left with no notice, and there were no clear reasons given for his departure. He had personally but briefly told each of the employees that he was leaving, proceeded to clean out his office, and was gone the same day.

The staff was suddenly left without a leader, as one employee stated. The president of the company, George Brown, called a meeting of the staff and announced that he was putting Linda Stevens, the assistant manager, in charge until a replacement could be found. There was no question of Linda permanently taking the job because she did not have the necessary managerial skills, nor was she entirely familiar with all the specific areas of the department. She was assistant manager more by virtue of having seniority and the most general knowledge of the department.

Linda was friends with most of the staff, particularly Margaret Wright. She knew that she could not be too assertive with staff members, especially Margaret, or she would be resented. She was fortunate in that everyone knew their job well and was responsible enough to get their work done on a short-term basis with minimal supervision. Her main responsibility would be to act as liaison between Mr. Brown and the staff and to assure him that the work was being done. Mr. Brown, by his own admission, knew little about accounting, so communications with the department were strained at times.

In addition to her liaison role, Linda was also expected to assume such duties as approving expense reports and, in general, coordinating efforts with

Southern's three other departments—sales, credit, and collections. The sales personnel worked out of offices in Virginia and North Carolina and, as expected, were constantly searching for new customers as well as maintaining relations with established clients. The credit department was responsible for approving and documenting new business as well as putting the information into the computer. Finally, the collections department, which consisted of one employee, John Howard, was primarily responsible for collecting past-due payments from the customers.

Linda's approach to dealing with the three departments was much more informal than that of the previous manager. If John needed information from the computer, she had him go directly to Margaret instead of going through her. She felt this eliminated an unnecessary step. It also necessitated better communications between Margaret and herself, because Linda still needed to be sure the work was completed. Nevertheless, this arrangement created some confusion as to whether anyone was clearly in charge of the department.

Linda was given Tom Johnson's work in addition to her own. Although his duties were not difficult and Linda had performed several of them in the past, she was pressed to do them and complete her own work. At the time the manager left, the computer had been down for three weeks, causing a backlog in the daily work. There were accounts to be reconciled, the corporate budget was due for revision, and there were sales tax reports to review and be filed. Linda needed to rely on the support of the staff and delegate as many of the duties as possible.

The previous "rules" of the department were broken at this time. Tom had insisted on having all information pass through him before it was presented to Mr. Brown. He would review it and then present it himself to Mr. Brown. Linda, realizing that she did not have the knowledge others had of their jobs, had the employees themselves go to Mr. Brown. She felt they could give him the information more accurately than she could. She also felt that there should be more effective communications between Mr. Brown and the staff and that there was a need at this time for mutual trust and support on both sides.

The staff managed to get the backlogged work caught up in the first week without an "official" manager. Linda, however, felt she needed help to finish her own work, so Mr. Brown called in Susan Tolbert, a former staff member who was now in another position in the company. Susan had been the previous assistant manager and was the only employee who had more seniority and experience than Linda.

It was Linda's understanding that Susan would be brought in to help out, since the month-end closing was approaching. Mr. Brown, however, put Susan "in charge" when she arrived, and this created some resentment at first on Linda's part. While she was not entirely at ease with the administrative side of the job, Linda and the staff had managed to get the work done. She had also, for the first time, felt comfortable with Mr. Brown and had begun to develop a rapport. In addition, this created some confusion for the staff and the rest of the company as to who was in charge. The reviewing duties assumed by Linda now fell on Susan.

There was the potential for a great deal of stress since it was known that Susan was being considered for the manager's position, and the fear was that she would use this time to prove her skills as manager by "telling the employees what to do." Some of the other staff members, like Linda, had become accustomed to doing their work on their own and essentially not answering to anyone. Rather than having this result in chaos, they had worked together as a whole and accomplished a great deal. There was a feeling of pride in the work that had not been present in the department for quite a while.

Susan, however, put everyone's mind at ease from the start. She was there, as she put it, to help out. She knew that everyone could do their job and do it on time. She also knew Linda needed help in order to do her own job and close out the month. She talked with Linda alone and they agreed on a division of duties agreeable to both. Susan would do the reviewing and administrative work while Linda would do her own job and review reports she had worked on before.

The staff was again in the position of being responsible for themselves. Under Tom, they had a manager who had made decisions based on his own perceptions without taking others' viewpoints into consideration. The basis for a decision would be that he "wanted it done his way!" The employees had felt that he did not entirely understand their jobs and made decisions more for expediency's sake. The answers given by Tom to Mr. Brown were often at odds with what the employees were doing. Because there was no direct line to Mr. Brown, they felt their viewpoints were somewhat distorted.

Due to the problems they had with Tom, the staff was leery about being under a new manager. Susan took her name out of consideration, so they figured they would get someone from outside the company. They also realized that Mr. Brown wanted someone to fill the vacancy as soon as possible. He needed one person he could talk to who would summarize the activities of the department since he felt uncomfortable dealing with the staff as a whole.

There were various opinions as to what type of manager was needed. The employees in the higher levels of the department wanted someone who would listen to their opinions before making a decision. They were looking for a degree of autonomy in their work and saw the need of a coordinator and organizer. They also felt they knew their jobs and it would be difficult to have a new manager who did not understand what they were doing. On the other hand, the employees in the clerical areas needed more guidance. They required a "leader" who would set limits and make the decisions. There was a small number of employees on the staff who fit this latter category, each having separate areas of responsibility.

One employee was responsible for posting the daily work, recording the checks that were received, and paying the bills. The job was clerical in nature, and it was the backbone of the department. The employee who held this job, Sarah Smith, was an older woman who was used to, and preferred, the guidance of a manager. She knew her job and was organized, but she was limited in her skills and therefore needed to have someone to instruct her when special situations arose. She did not like making her own decisions unless it fell within the routine of her job.

Another employee handled all the tax work including sales taxes, property taxes, and income taxes. Martha Carlton, 20, was the newest and youngest employee and this was her first full-time job. She had a degree in accounting and was bright, but when told she had to perform a certain duty, she would sometimes react by noting, "I don't want to do that." She needed close supervision to ensure her work was done and someone she could respect as a manager. She did not have this respect for Linda.

Margaret Wright was in charge of the computer operations and had been involved in the conversion to the new system being used. Next to Susan, Margaret knew more about the computer than anyone else and was used to implementing changes on her own. She knew that the company relied heavily on the computer and that she was in a position to implement the changes without the need for close supervision. Therefore, she felt that a manager was needed more to coordinate activities rather than to "sit on" the employees.

Mark Brady, the only male on the staff, was responsible for the analysis of accounts, preparation of financial statements, and working on the budget. He had a degree in finance and, like Margaret, was a self-starter. He had worked on taxes before and had proved himself in that area, having organized the taxes into a "workable situation."

He was becoming comfortable with his new duties and needed help primarily with unusual problems and new situations in which he had no experience. Like Margaret, Mark was looking for a manager who had faith in his work and would primarily act in a coordinating capacity.

Linda, like Margaret and Mark, liked doing her assigned work on her own. She knew what needed to be done but, unfortunately, lacked the organizational skills the others had. She worked more instinctively and tended to look to others for support. However, during the time she was without a manager, she had been acquiring some of the skills necessary to both finish the work and direct the staff.

Mr. Brown was in the process of interviewing candidates for the manager's position. He had Linda, Margaret, and Susan talk to each person he felt was worth consideration. He took their opinions into account, but everyone was aware that the final decision was his alone. There was a feeling of uneasiness among the staff as to what kind of manager they would have and how they would react to him. They were afraid that Mr. Brown would not take sufficient time to find someone, as he was eager to have the position filled. They now awaited his decision.

QUESTIONS

1. Should Linda take a firmer stand with the staff and be more of a formal leader, or was her informal style the most effective way of dealing with the present situation? Why?

2. Did Mr. Brown have to make a quick decision on hiring a manager or had the staff proved they could work without a formal manager as long as necessary?

3. What kind of manager would be best suited for this position?

12

EXCO MANUFACTURING COMPANY

"Come on Ray, I'm your wife, tell me what's bugging you. You've been moping around for a couple of days now."

"Well, I was talking to Ed, you know, the head of maintenance planning at the plant, and he happened to mention that the material coordinator position is a grade 24."

"I don't understand."

"Well, the material coordinator job doesn't require the qualifications nor the responsibilities that my job does and my job's only a grade 23!"

RAY MCKENZIE, PURCHASING AGENT

Ray McKenzie is a purchasing agent in the operations division of EXCO Manufacturing Company, a large firm based on the east coast. Although administratively responsible to the manager of purchasing in the corporate headquarters, he reports on a daily basis to his plant manager and is responsible for the procurement of all materials and services required for maintenance and operations within the plant.

In fulfilling his responsibilities, Ray works closely with the maintenance planning department, especially Jim Camp, the material coordinator. (See Figure 12.1.) Jim is responsible for reviewing material lists developed by the planners in order to determine which materials are already on hand (stock) and which materials must be purchased. Requisitions for required mate-

111

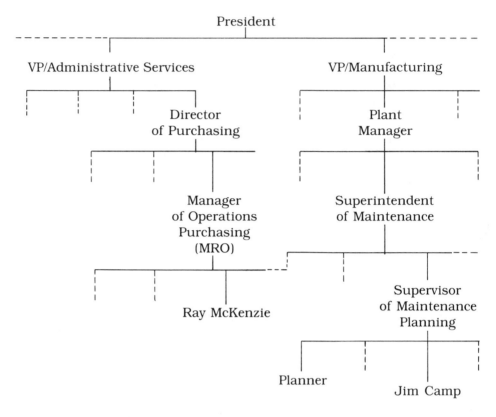

FIGURE 12.1 EXCO Manufacturing Company organizational chart

rials that have to be purchased are then forwarded to Ray for procurement.

When Ray came to EXCO two years ago, he brought with him three years of business experience and an undergraduate degree in business administration. He had started as an assistant purchasing agent in the corporate office but, with a lot of hard work, had been promoted to a purchasing agent in just over one year.

After several months in this capacity, he was selected to organize the first on-site purchasing operation at one of the company's nearby plants. Until this time all MRO purchasing had been done out of a single, central office located at corporate headquarters.

Although the new responsibilities did not involve an immediate promotion, Ray recognized the potential opportunity as this organizational change was part of a larger effort by the company to establish each of the manufacturing facilities as their own profit center. Besides the purchasing function, engineering, planning, and accounting functions were also being established at each of the plants.

JIM CAMP, MATERIAL COORDINATOR

Jim Camp had held a couple of brief construction jobs before joining EXCO almost three years ago. With limited experience and only a high school diploma, he had taken a job with the plant's labor gang. While performing the varied, menial tasks required in his job as a laborer, Jim became familiar with much of the equipment and with many of the people responsible for its operation and maintenance. In time, he became an apprentice and subsequently an assistant mechanic.

About six months ago, having demonstrated good mechanical ability and motivation, Jim was selected to be the material coordinator in the newly formed maintenance planning department. Although somewhat apprehensive about working behind a desk, Jim adjusted quickly and soon became quite proficient in his new capacity.

RELATIONS BETWEEN PURCHASING AND MAINTENANCE PLANNING

Ray started work at the plant shortly after the maintenance planning group began operations. At first, most of his time was spent familiarizing himself with the people and operations of the plant and then with organizing the purchasing operations. As the months went by, Ray began to take on more and more of the actual procurement function. Although requests for materials and services were generated by every department at the plant, the bulk of the requests came through the storeroom or maintenance planning department.

As Ray's office was located across the hall from the planning group, he became quite familiar with everyone in the group, especially the supervisor, Ed Baker. It was during one of his many discussions with Ed that Ray found out about some discrepancies in grade levels between his job and those of the planning group. Ray was quite disturbed since he believed that his job involved much more responsibility than those of the material coordinator or planners. However, he attributed the discrepancies to the fact that the jobs were relatively new and that the personnel department had simply made an error when establishing grade levels.

Regardless of the reason, Ray felt that the matter should be brought to the attention of management. However, he realized he must have more documentation of the problem before bringing it to management. He then contacted the purchasing agents at the other plants and found that the same situation existed throughout the system. With their help, he was able to obtain information concerning the job descriptions and grade levels of the relevant positions.

Armed with this information and the support of his peers, Ray presented his findings first to his man-

114

ager and then to the director of purchasing. In both instances, management listened politely, but without the interest that Ray had expected. The director of purchasing assured Ray that he had taken the correct action and that he would, in turn, present the findings to the personnel department for resolution as called for by company procedures.

Now, several months later, Ray had still not heard back from his manager or the personnel department, and he wondered whether the company was really interested in the concerns of its employees.

QUESTIONS

1. What was the basis for Ray's interest concerning the apparent discrepancies in grade levels?

2. If the pay grade situation had been reversed (i.e., Ray's grade level being higher than the others), would Ray's reaction have been different?

3. What are the potential consequences of management's continued inaction in this case?

13

UNITED NATIONAL BANK: AUDIT DEPARTMENT

Approximately three years ago, Bill Thomas was appointed to the position of general auditor by the Board of Directors of the United National Bank. This appointment set two precedents, with Bill not being a previous bank employee and the fact that he was a certified public accountant with extensive public accounting experience. Prior general auditors had been "home grown," and none of them had been professional accountants or auditors. Reporting directly to Mr. Thomas were the assistant general auditor, Sam Smith, and the audit manager, Jim Johnson (Figure 13.1).

As a professional, Bill quickly recognized many weaknesses within the department. However, the two areas that caused him the greatest concern were the quality of the present staff and the lack of audit attention being given to the data processing areas in the bank. In the past, the audit department had been staffed primarily from operating departments within the bank. Whereas the present staff was considered both competent and effective, few staff members were college graduates and most had not taken either accounting or auditing courses. In short, the staff did not possess the requisite skills that Mr. Thomas considered necessary to conduct the innovative types of audits he had been accustomed to in the public accounting environment. His second area of concern was the lack of audit attention given to electronic data processing (EDP) areas. He fully recognized that as the bank became increasingly automated, the audit staff would have to allocate a greater proportion of its personnel to auditing the computer and the related data processing functions.

In order to solve these problems, Mr. Thomas de-

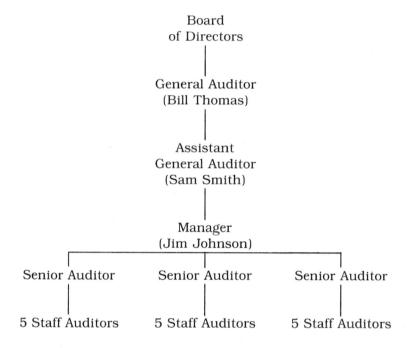

FIGURE 13.1 Organization chart (before EDP staff)

cided that he would have to upgrade the overall educational level of the staff by offering them training and educational opportunities, by hiring well-qualified individuals from outside the bank, and by establishing an EDP audit section in the department.

In establishing the EDP audit function, Bill created an EDP audit manager position (reporting directly to Sam Smith) and five other audit positions (Figure 13.2). The responsibilities of the EDP manager were to be limited to developing, implementing, and maintaining a quality EDP audit function. This individual would be spared many of the administrative duties such as budget preparation and secretarial supervision traditionally assigned to Jim Johnson. At this time,

Jim's title was changed from audit manager to financial audit manager. A separate area in the department was set aside for the EDP staff.

In staffing the EDP audit function, Mr. Thomas hired Bob Morrison, a data processing manager from a competing bank. Bob had previously worked for United National and was well known throughout the bank.

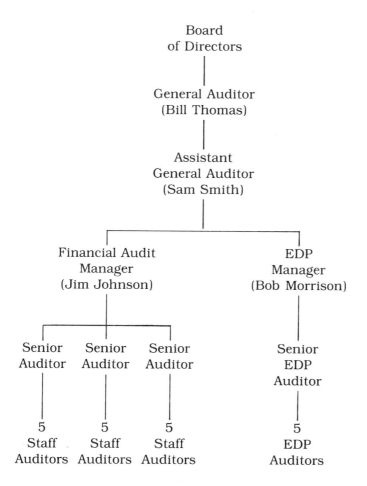

FIGURE 13.2 Organizational chart (after EDP staff)

While generally respected, he was considered by many, including Sam Smith and Jim Johnson, to be a mover and smooth talker. The remaining five positions on the EDP staff were filled over a period of three years by people from outside the bank and from within United National, all of whom had data processing and audit experience. No members of the present staff were considered by either Mr. Thomas or Bob to possess the necessary educational skills or practical experience to fill the positions.

When filling the EDP positions, Bill Thomas discovered that EDP auditors were in high demand in the marketplace. As a result, the salaries of the EDP staff at any given grade level were generally $2,000–$3,000 higher than those of the financial audit staff. This was true except in the case of Bob Morrison and Jim Johnson. Bob's salary was approximately $2,000 less than Jim's. Mr. Thomas justified this because he said that Jim performed additional administrative duties and had been employed by the bank for a longer period of time.

During the time that the EDP staff was being established, changes were also taking place on the financial audit staff. Two employees had transferred to other departments in the bank at the insistence of Mr. Thomas, two had resigned, and three had retired. In each case, these employees were replaced by college graduates with degrees in accounting or finance and several had MBA degrees or were CPA's.

The staff in general had been strongly encouraged to take advantage of evening courses offered at local universities that were paid for by the bank. The importance of continuing education was stressed by Mr. Thomas when he stated during a staff meeting: "Over the next ten years, I expect the audit profession to change dramatically. The environment in which we work has become very technical due to the rapid implementation of automated systems. We must be prepared to meet the challenge. I have two options. Number one, I can hire a staff with the necessary skills. Or, number two, I can make the resources available for each of you to upgrade your present skills as necessary. I have chosen the latter course. The rest is up to you. I trust I will not be disappointed."

Mr. Thomas' message was received loud and clear, and a majority of the financial staff began taking courses in accounting, auditing, and data processing. This placed a particular burden on the older employees (those hired before Mr. Thomas's appointment) since for the most part they had been away from school for many years and few had taken college courses. These older employees also recognized that while they had on-the-job experience, Mr. Thomas and his management team were grooming the newer employees to assume future management positions.

During the first two years of existence, the EDP staff concentrated on developing and conducting audits in the data processing areas of the bank. As a result, contact between the EDP and financial staffs was somewhat limited. There was some minimal contact for business and social reasons, but, by and large, the two groups remained apart. There existed some resentment by the financial staff toward the EDP staff due to the salary differential and the prestige assigned to these auditors for their ability to audit computers and to converse in computer jargon. During one staff meeting, one of Jim's senior auditors commented: "I get along fine with those people away from the bank, but I can't stand to work with them. A computer science degree isn't a bit more difficult to earn than an accounting degree but they sure do think they're something special."

In addition, the EDP staff members had not gone out of their way to encourage a close relationship. After all, they were the specialists. Their interest in learning to audit cash, securities, or other valuables was less than enthusiastic. Anyone could count but not everyone could audit a computer! However, many of the traditional areas in the bank had recently begun to automate their work as evidenced by computer terminals and printouts beginning to appear with increased frequency. As a result, the financial staff began to rely upon the EDP auditors for assistance in auditing the automated activities. This encouraged cooperation between the groups, but increased the workload of the EDP auditors. This also served to strengthen the EDP auditors' feeling of importance to the department.

Ill feelings between the financial and EDP staffs also extended to the management level. Jim Johnson was less than pleased when he heard of Bob Morrison's employment at the bank. He and Bob had previously worked in the same department in the bank and were not fond of one another. Consequently, Jim was not looking forward to working with Bob again. At the same time, while Bob felt that he had been given sufficient latitude to develop the EDP program, he was worried about the amount of influence Jim had on Sam and the entire department—including the EDP staff. Although Bob had considered himself to be an easygoing sort who liked to avoid confrontation where possible, he felt the time had come to have a chat with Sam Smith, the assistant general auditor. The following exchange occurred:

Bob: You know Sam, I'm aware of what's going on around here and I'm getting sick and tired of it. Everytime I turn around, you and Jim are making decisions that impact this department. I'm the last to know, and rarely do I have the opportunity to comment, and then it seems that I'm on the wrong side of the fence. The EDP staff is an important part of this department and I don't appreciate the two of you making decisions that impact my staff. Just the other day, Jim sent that memo to the staff concerning the assignments on the next securities audit. Those assignments affect my staff and we're already behind schedule. We don't mind helping, but I sure would like to know about it in advance. That memo should have come from Jim and me.

Sam: Bob, I just don't know how you can say those things! I try to keep you informed of all major decisions and don't forget those Monday morning staff meetings I have with both you and Jim. If that's not communicating, I don't know what is. Furthermore, I think you're being unfair to Jim. I'll admit that he should have contacted you, but he's got a lot of additional responsibilities that you don't have. He can't always afford to have you completely involved. Just look at the hours he spends here. Jim is a valuable employee.

Bob: Well, I can see that I'm not getting anywhere with this conversation. The problem is that you and Jim think too much alike. And another thing, the reason he's so busy is that he works harder, not smarter. He must get that big salary for being inefficient. I guess Jim's the fair-haired boy around here and I'll just have to accept that. Let's change the subject. As you're aware, the EDP staff is having to spend an increasing amount of time helping the financial staff with their audits. This is putting us behind schedule and something has to give. You've got some bright young folks on the financial staff, and I think they should be able to assume some of our less technical tasks such as auditing the automated systems in their areas. After all, some of the financial staff members have been taking EDP classes at night and they're anxious to put that knowledge to work.

Sam: Bob, I think that's an excellent idea. Let me talk it over with Jim and we'll get back with you.

Sam relayed his entire conversation with Bob to Jim. Jim agreed by responding, "That's just fine with me. You know I'm always ready to accept a new challenge and besides, this will help prove my theory that EDP auditing isn't all that difficult. But you know, I don't trust Bob for a minute. I can't believe he said those things about me. You never know what a guy like him will say next. Let me give him a call. We should all let Bill know what we're planning to do."

"I agree," replied Sam. "Also Jim, I want you to know that I support you 100 percent."

QUESTIONS

1. What appears to be the most significant problem facing Bill Thomas and the audit department?

2. What would be the most efficient way(s) of handling the problems?

14

ADKINS TEA COMPANY

The Adkins Tea Company was founded in 1940 with a simple idea and a small group of hard-working individuals. At that time there were only three major tea companies, with Adkins being a comparatively small newcomer. Ever since its inception the company has been extremely innovative. Starting with one plant located in the East, its hard work, efficient operations, and skilled managers turned scarce resources into large profits. The tea company reinvested its profits and began to expand. In 1975, with three plants already existing, Adkins opened the largest tea processing plant in the world. From 1975 to the present, domestic and export sales have doubled and now Adkins is the largest tea manufacturer in the world. The company recently instigated a diversification program that has created additional expansion as well as profit.

Adkins has a large product line with more than 15 brands of tea that are sold internationally. Production is a process consisting of primary and fabrication stages. In the primary stage the raw tea leaves are brought to the plant in hogsheads and are stripped and combined with different flavor blends. Moisture is then added, and the blended tea is pumped by pipes up through the basement to the fabrication process. This area is composed of 120 tea machines that are grouped by tea type and packaging form. The tea is run through the machines and is placed in either tea bags or tea containers. This process has been revolutionized to the point where the four plants produce over two billion tea bags/containers a day. Over the years Adkins has developed staff groups to control and reduce operating costs, with the customer service group having expanded the most in recent years.

CUSTOMER SERVICE DEPARTMENT

The customer service department is composed of 20 service representatives, four supervisors, an office manager, and a departmental manager. In brief, this group serves as a liaison among the customers, sales personnel, and manufacturing operations. Because of the company's rapid growth and top management's need for more detailed reporting of transactions, complaints, etc., customer service has been performing under the most severe time constraints. A great deal of the work is done manually since the computer system is very ineffective at times. Accordingly, both motivation and morale within the department fluctuate.

The current strength of the department is found in its four supervisors. These individuals are aggressive, young professionals, all of whom are working on MBA degrees. In addition, the department manager, Bob Harris, is a well-respected leader in the department and is always open to recommendations or criticisms emanating from his four supervisors. With such a climate, the group is considered highly productive, creative, and cohesive. Representatives have been given responsibility and a chance to develop by taking on a variety of tasks and finding more efficient ways to perform their current jobs. The vertical channels of communication are open with any feedback being very constructive and taken in a positive manner.

The center of attention in the department deals with the position of office manager. Ordinarily, this position operates in a liaison role between the supervisors and department manager and, in general, is responsible for the short-run activities as well as relieving some of Bob Harris' workload. This position has been vacant for about three months as a result of the untimely death of Pete Jenkins. The supervisors indicate that there is really no need for an office manager at this time. However, they also agree that the position could provide a good training ground for a future department manager.

THE NEW OFFICE MANAGER

Due in part to Adkins' commitment to a strong affirmative action program, Roy Smith was appointed the new office manager in customer service. Smith, a black, had no previous experience in customer service or inside sales operations but was being cross-trained to fill a requirement in upper management. His initial attitude toward the supervisors in the group was an open, friendly one due to his inexperience. After an initial apprehension toward Smith, the supervisors began to accept his appointment. The friendly relationship, though, began to deteriorate rapidly after Smith learned the system and his true leadership style emerged. In short, a democratic approach to leadership in the office was replaced by one of authoritarianism. The vertical channel of communication between the representatives, supervisors, and the department manager now came through the office manager and was distorted based on what Smith felt his subordinates should know. Smith's autocratic rule carried over into every aspect of the subordinates' job. Suggestions on new approaches or shortcuts to better results were discouraged time and again by Smith. He also curtailed the job freedom that had previously existed by demanding that the subordinates fill out time sheets listing every hour spent in their day.

At this time, several service representatives were due for a performance appraisal. The traditional policy at Adkins is that an employee receives a monetary increase at least once a year, with the appraisal being completed two months before the increase. The office manager was required to fill out an appraisal form showing the weight given to each aspect of the employees' job functions. Smith's performance appraisals were consistent with his autocratic style. The subordinate was brought into his office for a closed door session in which Smith presented a brief overview of the employees' past year's work. Smith's train of thought throughout the session was rather negative and discouraging. He highlighted the employees' weaknesses and downplayed their strengths while allowing only minimal participation by the subordinate. Smith raced through the review, providing very subjective thoughts on past performance. Typically, an employee was given a mediocre grade at best because Smith felt that no one could be considered exceptional. This attitude was not only unmotivating to the group but also inconsistent with the views of other supervisors in the department.

Currently, morale in the group is very low, motivation is down, and the only saving grace is the cohesiveness of the group. The department manager has only recently been made aware of the declining situation while the office manager has consistently placed the blame on the group rather than examine his leadership style. In order to get a better picture of what is occurring, the department manager decided to have some informal discussions with the supervisors. Bob Harris is now beginning to "see the light" and must decide what he should do with Roy Smith.

QUESTIONS

1. What barriers to effective communication exist within the department and what impact do these barriers have on the solution to the current situation?

2. What could Smith have done to ease the friction between himself and the supervisors (and subordinates)?

3. What are the alternative courses of action available to the department manager for dealing with Smith?

15

BROOKSTONE PLANT: ENGINEERING GROUP

Mike Danvers, the chief engineer at Skyline Structures' Brookstone Plant, was conducting his weekly department meeting with his lead design engineers. Unlike the usual conversation pertaining to relevant scheduling and technical information, the subject of this meeting was reserved for other matters.

In recent weeks, Mike had been informed by several members of his engineering section that morale was steadily decreasing. He was aware of this situation because of increased scheduling difficulties due to reductions in worker output. Also, conflict among group members was becoming noticeably stronger. Therefore, it was Mike's intent to utilize this meeting as a forum to determine the factors causing this situation, and the proposal of viable options to relieve it.

COMPANY BACKGROUND

Skyline Structures is one of the largest manufacturers of prestressed and architectural precast concrete in the country. As a subsidiary of a major retailing conglomerate, Skyline has built a network of precast concrete fabricating plants across the western half of the United States. Operations at any plant involve the manufacturing of concrete structural components. Once hardened, they are transported to a construction site where they are assembled to produce the intended structure. Construction has ranged from warehouses and bridges to multistory apartments, hotels, parking decks, and office structures. Profits for this type of engineering are mainly dependent on speed of production and repetition of product (multiple production of a particular piece).

PLANT BACKGROUND

The Brookstone Plant became part of Skyline Structures network in 1976 and was in operation for 15 years prior to its acquisition. Typical for each plant in the network, the Brookstone Plant maintains its own complete engineering, production, and support capabilities (Figure 15.1). As required, additional financial and technical services are available from the Plattsville Plant, which serves as headquarters for Skyline Structures.

The Brookstone Plant is currently in a period of significant growth. Since its acquisition, the intent had been to continue expansion as rapidly as possible to

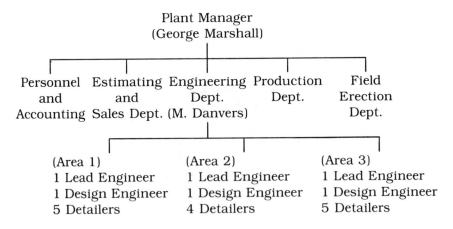

Figure 15.1   Brookstone Plant organization chart

take advantage of a strong construction market. To keep abreast of increased production necessary to meet the demands of the market, the support (staff) groups have also required expansion. The greatest impact has been with the engineering department. Since 1976, the total number of engineers has increased from two to six. The drafting group, which is part of the engineering section, has increased from five to 14 employees.

ENGINEERING DEPARTMENT PERSONNEL

Following is a brief profile of several key employees closely involved in the day-to-day operations of the engineering section:

George Marshall, plant manager, was hired at his present position after the plant was acquired by Skyline Structures in 1976. With 23 years experience in the industry, his main responsibility has been to provide a successful expansion program for the plant. His experience has ranged from sales to engineering (registered engineer in several states) to production for several major precast concrete manufacturers throughout the country. His current role includes an active and dominant role in all phases of the Brookstone operation.

Mike Danvers, the chief engineer, was in this same position prior to the plant's acquisition. Born and raised in Brookstone, he is well known in the engineering community for leadership in his profession. At the age of 36, his technical expertise in the company's products is well proven. Therefore, he was asked to continue at his present job with the new management team, and realizing the potential growth of the firm, he accepted the challenge.

Dan Forbes, a lead design engineer, has been with the plant just over two years. His high level of technical expertise makes him well qualified to complete the design aspects demanded by his job. Once assigned to a project, he is given engineering control from initial design to completion of the design drawings (which are necessary to manufacture and erect the structure). Only unusual or highly sophisticated design problems require consultation with Mike or George prior to a job's completion. On nontechnical problems, task completion normally requires direct consultation with the sales and production managers within the plant and the outside architects and engineers. Don, like the other engineers, is in his mid- to late 20's and has been idealistic about what the future will offer him at Brookstone.

MEETINGS WITH SUBORDINATES

Although signs of problems with the operation of Mike's group were appearing, he was not clear as to the extent of the situation until he had completed candid discussions with Don and two of the draftsmen in his department.

Among the engineers, salary had been the prime topic for discussion. As the company grew in sales and production, so did the engineers' responsibilities to their jobs. Work hours were now averaging nine per weekday, minimum half-day on Saturday, and time on Sunday when necessary. Don, like his peers, felt he had accepted his position at a salary below what he felt was desirable because of the growth potential. However, as each raise was presented, Mike indicated that management was not showing a profit. This meant raises had been kept below seven percent (annual) for each of the last two reviews. Moreover, all performance reviews were informal, as were job descriptions on which these appraisals were based.

Schedules were becoming more demanding as expansion continued to increase workloads. Hiring additional employees always seemed to lag, creating constant staffing deficiencies. As schedules tightened, tension between the engineering and production staff heightened, since late schedules meant loss of production time.

The engineer's drafting group was also experiencing behavioral problems. Unlike the engineers, they were paid on an hourly rather than a salary basis. The recent move by all plant support groups, including engineering, to a new office had enhanced the poor working conditions previously felt by the detailers. However, this alone did not appear to be sufficient to eliminate complaints. This group averaged 22 years in age and worked in an open area arrangement. They were in all stages of job development in terms of job skills. Another significant consideration at this time is the fact that opportunities with other companies in the Brookstone area are minimal. Because of this factor, many are not voicing their opinions about this situation to their supervisors due to possible adverse repercussions.

QUESTIONS

1. What factors have created the problems of the employees contained in Mike's engineering department?

2. How can Mike resolve these situations and develop a more meaningful and productive environment for these individuals?

3. What alternate approaches could the chief engineer institute if the solution in question (2) is later discovered to be ineffective?

16

STATE DEPARTMENT OF REVENUE: OFFICE SERVICES DIVISION

The state department of revenue was organized in 1920 with Cyrus Clark being appointed state revenue commissioner and serving in that capacity until his retirement in 1970. During his 50-year tenure, the department's employment rolls increased from 60 to 750 employees. Following his retirement, Mr. Bob Franklin was appointed commissioner and still holds that position today. Bob is very authoritative and has great influence over his managers.

In 1971 there were three divisions reporting directly to the state revenue commissioner. During Franklin's 12-year tenure the department has undergone several major organizational changes and is currently organized by function with several major divisions, each of which is ultimately responsible to one of the two deputy state revenue commissioners or the state revenue commissioner. The department is organized into three submanagement teams as follows: the office of the commissioner, which includes the state revenue commissioner, the two deputy state revenue commissioners, and the tax policy division; the office of administrative operations, consisting of one of the deputy commissioners and the heads of staff services within the agency; and the office of tax operations, composed of the other deputy commissioner and the directors of line and field service functions (see Figure 16.1).

In team decision making at the top level, the three offices (or management team) collectively provide input into the decision process. Once a consensus has been reached, it is recommended to the state revenue commissioner as the best course of action to be followed relative to the situation or issue that initiated the pro-

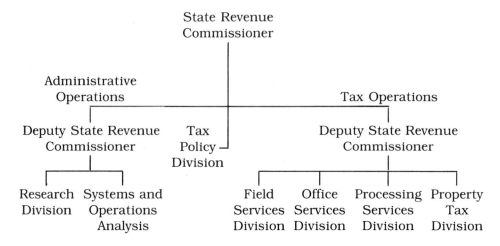

Figure 16.1 Management team: Office of the commissioner

cess. Whereas the commissioner serves as part of the management team by virtue of his membership in the office of the commissioner, he must make the final decision because of the necessities of legislative authority, responsibility, and accountability. The same process of team decision making is followed throughout all levels of the agency along with the use of management by objectives (MBO).

Using the MBO concept, the management team establishes objectives for the department as a whole, taking into account the specific objectives set for the offices of administrative operations and tax operations by their management teams. By the same account, objectives established on supervisory and divisional levels are considered when the objectives for each office are determined. Objectives and accomplishments are reviewed quarterly on a department-wide basis and, more frequently, on the divisional level.

THE OFFICE SERVICES DIVISION

The office services division solicits payments of delinquent taxes through office collection methods (collections section), renders taxpayer assistance (taxpayer assistance section), and conducts office audits including office compliance programs along with assigning field audits (compliance section). The division director is Floyd Lawson, who has been with the department for about 20 years and has risen up through the ranks. Although having the responsibility for the planning and controlling of the office services division, Floyd has been considered a weak link in the office of tax operations' management team. He does not get along well with the state revenue commissioner and many of the other directors. Also, it has long been acknowledged that he has a drinking problem.

The assistant director of the division is Elliot Hammer, who has 35 years service with the department and is only three years from retirement. He is responsible primarily for the daily operations of the division. Although he has held a variety of management positions, Elliot has always been passed over for the director's job. Speculation among the division employees is that Elliot also has a drinking problem, and this has been a significant factor in preventing Elliot from reaching the top.

The supervisor of the taxpayer assistance section is Ralph Worthy. He's been with the department for about 20 years, and he too has risen up through the ranks. He previously worked for Floyd before the department was reorganized functionally three years ago. However, Ralph's section is still operating under an inefficient setup, with the examiners specializing in only one tax area. Ralph has been known to promote people according to years of service rather than ability;

thus the section is composed of employees who have been with the department for many years. In addition, there are no written operating procedures and thus many examiners are free-lancing with their work. This has caused a constant backlog of work in the individual tax area, whereas the business tax area examiners are not busy enough. Ralph is constantly telling Floyd that he doesn't have enough workers and that he never knows how many office audits the compliance section will be generating. Many of the employees in the section are disgruntled over the situation, with morale and production running very low.

The collections section is headed by Chris Downing, who's been with the department for about 10 years. He is a former Marine sergeant and his management style reflects this. He is considered a workaholic, and all types of decisions must pass over his desk. Such an atmosphere has created a very tense setting, thus contributing to the existence of low morale and falling production. He, too, is constantly telling Floyd that he's short of personnel.

The compliance section has experienced the most rapid growth in the last eight years. Due to new tax laws, 15 college graduates have been added to work on new programs. The section is headed by Joe Grimes, who has been with the department for about 15 years. Like the other sectional supervisors, Joe never went to college and has risen up through the ranks of the department by paying his dues. He also is known to have a drinking problem, and on many occasions has taken three-hour liquid lunches. To make matters worse, he has occasionally failed to return to the office after lunch. Recently these lunches have started to include the assistant supervisor and some of his subordinates. The other assistant supervisor doesn't join in on these lunches and many times has had to cover for the missing persons. Also, the other subordinates, who don't go to these lunches, have become disgruntled and want to know why this practice is continued.

Jerry Noland is the assistant supervisor (Joe's drinking partner) and has been with the department for about 10 years. He too, did not go to college and has risen up through the department. He was promoted by Joe over candidates who appeared to be more qualified into his present position last year. Since Jerry has taken over, a motivation problem has started to emerge among the younger workers. In setting objectives for the section, Joe and Jerry have set rather low assessment figures that are easily attainable in order for the section to look good. Thus many of the young workers (college graduates) have slacked off in their production since there are no incentives to produce more. They know if they meet the minimum standards they'll get their merit pay increase. Meanwhile, the older workers are content just to do as they are told and work at their own pace.

Every Wednesday, Floyd and Elliot meet with their three sectional supervisors to discuss issues. The following conversation occurred in the most recent meeting:

Floyd: At last week's management team meeting, Commissioner Franklin stated that the department will be developing a new computer system, which will increase efficiency by eliminating a lot of time-consuming manual operations. Also each division's budget would be cut 5 percent to help defray the cost of the project.

Ralph: That's great *(sarcastically).* I need more employees and now they want to cut back! Also, those computer systems never work. It looks like they cause more harm than good. What's wrong with the way things are now?

Chris: I agree with Ralph. What's wrong with the present system? This new system will probably flop like previous systems.

Joe: Floyd, I see their points. Everytime the systems and operations analysis division introduces a new computer system we are also left in the dark. We never know what's going on. Most of the time the printouts we receive from them are incorrect, and they always tell us that they don't have time to correct them.

Floyd: Ok, I'll see what I can do. Any other problems?

Joe: I met with Byron Hunt *(supervisor in the field services division)* to discuss problems about certain field audits we've assigned to them that they won't audit, because they aren't profitable. The problem lies in the fact that their objective for the fiscal year is to assess $4 million in field audits, whereas our objective in assigning field audits is to produce voluntary compliance and not revenue.

Ralph: Have any of you been experiencing absenteeism problems lately?

Joe: Funny you should mention it, but I've seen an increase in our section.

Chris: Same with me.

Joe: Hey Elliot, have you checked on those parking spaces near the building for Stan and Bob *(two examiners in his section)*? They keep complaining to me that they've been here for 20 years and can't even get a space near the building, whereas the secretaries for top management do.

Floyd (to Ralph):   The deputy commissioner told me he's been getting complaints from taxpayers who can't get through on the lines.

Ralph: As you know, the examiners have to answer the phones and also have to work on written correspondence. We've got such a backlog of cases that sometimes we have to switch off the lines to catch up. Also, you know about our manpower shortage.

Floyd: Well gentlemen, if there's no other business let's go to lunch.

QUESTIONS

1. What are the major types of problems being experienced by the office services division? Why?

2. How could the MBO system be changed to eliminate (or even reduce) the problems being encountered within the division?

17

ABE LINCOLN WATER ASSOCIATION, INC.

The Abe Lincoln Water Association, Inc., chartered in December, 1976, was formed as a nonprofit organization for the purpose of providing and maintaining a water system for rural residents living generally south of Sand Hill, Illinois. Prior to the establishment of the association, individuals were forced to develop their own water source and delivery systems and to provide for system maintenance.

The association was formed primarily by Norm Smith, a local farmer, and his neighbor, Jim Dashford, an insurance agent in Sand Hill. The efforts of these two men resulted in some 15 families joining together to form the association.

The association obtained the necessary funds to begin its operation through federal grants and loans. The initial funds were used to employ a consulting engineering firm to construct the system and for working capital. Sources and application of these funds are shown in Table 17.1. The association began operations in April, 1978. The balance sheet at the end of the first nine months of operation indicated total assets at approximately $185,000 and total liabilities of $124,000.

Case prepared by Roy E. Carpenter, Professor of Management at Southeastern Louisiana University and reprinted with permission.

TABLE 17.1   Abe Lincoln Water Association, Inc.—statement of receipts and disbursements, construction account, for the 31 months ending December 31, 1978

RECEIPTS:

Bank Balance—June 1, 1978		-0-
Loan from Farmers Home Administration	$122,000.00	
Grant from United States Government	63,000.00	
Total Receipts		$185,000.00

DISBURSEMENTS:

Construction of Facilities	147,935.49	
Engineering Costs	10,353.40	
Legal Fees	2,000.00	
Prepaid Interest to F.H.A.	9,994.00	
Total Disbursements		$170,282.89
Bank Balance—December 31, 1978		$ 14,717.11

OPERATIONS

Currently, the association acts solely as a distributor of water purchased from the city of Sand Hill. (The purchase agreement between the association and city of Sand Hill is shown in Table 17.2.) Three main meters connect the association's system to the city water mains. City personnel read these meters monthly and bill the association for usage. Ray George, a local farmer, reads the meters of the association on or around the 20th of each month and records the reading on a meter book ledger sheet, which is then turned over to Bob Smith. Bob computes the water usage for each customer, calculates the bill, and mails the bills to the customers. The bills are calculated according to a variable billing rate. (The rate scale can be seen in Table 17.3.)

Both Bob Smith and Ray George are paid 50 cents per meter from the association as their compensation for these services.

In addition to reading meters, Ray George and his son, Jerry, perform maintenance work, install new meters, and remove meters when service is terminated.

TABLE 17.2   Water purchase rate agreement with city of Sand Hill

The System agrees to pay the City not later than the 25th day of each month* for water delivered in accordance with the following schedule of rates:

1. For water not exceeding 3,000 gallons—$3.00 per month, which sum is hereby fixed and established as the respective minimum rate for the use of water per month.
2. For water in excess of 3,000 gallons per month and not exceeding 5,000 gallons per month, Sixty Cents ($.60) per 1,000 gallons.
3. For water in excess of 5,000 gallons per month and not exceeding 10,000 gallons per month, Fifty-Five Cents ($.55) per 1,000 gallons.
4. For water in excess of 10,000 gallons and not exceeding 20,000 gallons per month, Fifty Cents ($.50) per 1,000 gallons per month.
5. For water in excess of 20,000 gallons per month and not exceeding 50,000 gallons per month, Forty Cents ($.40) per 1,000 gallons per month.
6. For water in excess of 50,000 gallons, but not exceeding 200,000 gallons per month, Thirty Cents ($.30) per 1,000 gallons per month.
7. For all water in excess of 200,000 gallons per month, Twenty Cents ($.20) per 1,000 gallons per month.

*The City reads the three main meters which connect the Lincoln System with the City System around the 10th of each month.

TABLE 17.3 Rates for members' water consumption

Rates for water consumption of the members of the Abe Lincoln Water System:

Installation	$150
0 to 2,000 gallons	$5
Next 2,000 gallons @ $1.00 per 1,000 gallons	
Next 3,000 gallons @ .75 per 1,000 gallons	
All over 10,000 gallons @ .50 per 1,000 gallons	
Minimum monthly bill	$5

They are paid $30 per meter installation or meter removal, and $6 per hour for general repair work. During 1981, Ray and Jerry averaged 12.5 hours each for general repair. Jerry would like to work full-time for the association if he could be guaranteed a minimum of $500 per month.

Customers who receive their bills on the first of each month are assessed a 10 percent late charge if they do not pay the bills within 10 days. Bills are paid at the Bank of Sand Hill. (The bank charges the association $40 per month for this service.) Service is pulled when an account is 60 days delinquent. However, no meter has ever been pulled for lack of payment. The association has had continued growth in its five years of operation. In fact, the number of customers has increased from 115 to 305. The system was originally engineered to provide water for approximately 200 customers, but continual requests for service required the installation of two booster stations in 1981 to maintain sufficient water pressure for the users. At the present time, the system is comprised of 29 miles of P.V.C. pipe ranging in size from 8-inch mains to 3/4-inch customer service lines.

THE FUTURE

Since the beginning, neither the city nor the association has increased their water rates although expenses have escalated. The association's board fears that the city of Sand Hill will soon, out of necessity, increase rates charged the association by 10 percent. Also, there is some concern that the city may terminate its agreement, especially if the association's growth places pressure on the city's well capacity. (The city may contractually terminate service by giving six months' notice.)

As a contingency, Norm Smith contracted with Latham Well-Drillers to study the system and to make recommendations as to location, size, well type, and storage system to efficiently serve the association's needs. Latham recommended a 12,000 gallon main storage tank and a system operating pressure of 70 psi. It was estimated that eight weeks would be required to complete the job. The initial cost of the project would be $108,000, but cost increases were estimated to be 1/2 percent per month thereafter. Latham's report was dated April, 1982. In addition, land acquisition would cost $2,200, and legal fees would total 3 percent of project costs. The Farmer's Home Administration felt that the association could obtain a $30,000 grant and finance 80 percent of the project's remaining cost at 8 1/2 percent over a 30-year period. Also, the current system is some five years old and has begun to have some leaks. Norm Smith estimates that leakage is between 6 and 10 percent of total monthly volume.

Norm Smith has decided that the relative complexity of the situation warrants the use of an outside consultant prior to making any recommendations to the board. When John Adamson of Kirschfield and Associates arrived from Chicago, the two men decided to tackle some of the key questions that would definitely be examined at the next board meeting.

QUESTIONS

1. Should the association consider hiring a full-time person for installation, meter reading, billing, and general repair? What salary would you pay this person if hired?

2. Should the association contract for the new well at this time or wait until the city of Sand Hill gives notice of termination of services?

3. What other problems should Norm Smith be concerned with?

18

CLIMATE COMPANY, INC.

Jim Newins, manager of branch operations for Climate Company, had just completed the third quarter review of 20 branches for which he was accountable. He was responsible for inventory control, forecasting, budget implementation, and operations problems. He was particularly satisfied with the results shown by the Washington Branch. The Washington operation had been a budget spoiler for many years, so it was with relief that Jim observed marked progress in all operational areas. The branch was on trend lines that would bring them to their year-end objectives.

Meanwhile, Sam Parker, vice-president of sales and marketing, was in the hot seat. Newly appointed in the past six months, he was reviewing a dismal sales record reflected by both the company-owned branches and the independent distributors that Climate sold to. Industry shipments for the major product lines were down for 1982 through the third quarter as much as 36 percent. Heat pump shipments, the third highest product by unit volume and second in dollar sales, were down 22 percent. Air conditioners, second highest by unit volume and first in dollar sales, were down 17 percent. The primary contribution to these conditions was high interest rates. They were having a double-barreled effect on his sales results. First, new construction was greatly off the rate that had carried housing starts to 2.3 million in 1979. The present year was shaping up at around 1 million starts. Secondly, his distributors and branches had reduced finished goods inventory to historically low levels. The cost of holding inventory was so high that the distribution outlets were forcing the responsibility of inventory on the factory by not ordering until a customer needed the product. These industry-wide problems were not expected to be present in all markets. Specifically, areas of high government employment or defense industries were to be the bright spots for both the construction industry and equipment manufacturers. It was with the anticipation of satisfactory performance in these markets that Sam Parker reviewed the sales performance of the Washington Branch in disbelief.

The Washington Branch, located in Maryland, had been created seven years ago through the merger of the two distribution outlets serving Washington and Baltimore. Both these locations had been in existence as long as the company itself. The Baltimore factory branch had been combined with the personnel from the independent distributor who had served the Washington market. The company had committed considerable resources to provide a modern distribution facility to serve this key market. Although company policy was to distribute through independent distribution wherever possible, an exception had been made for the Baltimore/Washington market. This was a result of the stability and expected continual growth available in this market.

The branch was staffed with long-time employees from the previous distributorships. Pete Child, the manager selected for this operation, was the eastern regional sales manager. Previously he had successfully held the position of territory manager (salesman) attached to the Baltimore office. His performance had been above average. From 1975 through 1981 he had brought sales volume from $3 million to $12 million. More importantly, he had increased market share to the level that was considered saturation. This performance was accomplished by the manager, in part, through his personal style, salesmanship, and relations with both employees and customers. He disdained paper work. This weakness was partially covered by both the operations manager and sales manager, who frequently completed managerial reports for him. Pete frequently accompanied salesmen on their calls and was liberal with their expense account allowances. Sales meetings always included a long, two-martini lunch with much storytelling. Vacation time for salesmen was never strictly accounted for. The frequent remark was, "As long as you're doing a good job selling, I don't know how many days you take off." In mid-season, when the warehouse and parts department was backlogged, Pete would be on the fork-lift loading trucks or behind the counter serving customers. Pete was able to extract loyalty from his customers.

Commitments for a season's business are made through negotiation with contractors. Negotiations not only include price, but the inclusion of customers on company-sponsored trips to Europe and other desirable locations. Customers sometimes purchased from the branch because of the hospitality and good times created for them by Pete. His customers went to the best restaurants, had the best seats at the dinner theater, etc. His stated philosophy was to consider people as personal friends and treat them accordingly. These relationships, policies, and expectations were developed over the seven years of his employment at the Washington branch. This came quickly to an end in mid-March of 1982. Because of a rumored salary dispute, Pete Child resigned and took immediate employment at a higher level with a major manufacturing competitor.

Immediately the company appointed a new manager, transferred from the California operation. The new manager, Neil Jones, took charge the following week. An unscheduled sales meeting was called with the message that past practices were no longer acceptable. The content of the meeting included references to gross mismanagement in the past by his predecessor.

Neil implied that future decisions would be made on sound business logic, not arbitrarily as in the past. The employees and salesmen were leery of the new manager, and this resulted in a degree of behavior modification. The lunch portion of the sales meeting took place with only the new manager having wine with his meal. All other employees uncharacteristically had soft drinks or iced tea. Under considerable stress were those employees who had nine years of service to the company and required an additional year to become vested for retirement.

The new manager brought immediate alienation to himself by constantly referring to California and the proper way in which policies and practices were followed at his previous location. Ten days into his new assignment, Neil ordered the coffee service discontinued, subscriptions to trade publications cancelled, the warehouse heat to be turned off, and promotional gift items (e.g., golf balls with company logo) locked in a closet. These actions promoted resentment from the affected parties. The office staff resented the removal of the coffee service, warehouse employees' productivity decreased, and the sales force felt untrusted. Additional dissatisfaction resulted from the introduction of sales quotas. Previously, salesmen were credited for parts purchases made by their accounts. New policy classified these sales as "house accounts." No corresponding adjustments were made to salesmen's quotas.

These initial changes were quickly related with negative connotations to the customers by employees in customer service and sales. Daily stories describing confrontations with customers and employees were passed through the grapevine. A typical example of a story on the new manager was that he had hung up the telephone on an important customer. Other insinuations were that he always reported to work after 9:00 a.m. while the business office opened at 7:30 a.m. Lastly, when customers or other employees inquired about him, office personnel would remark that they never saw him because he was always in his office with the door closed.

Following an initial 30-day stint, Neil returned to California for packing and moving. He opted to combine move time with vacation time, thereby leaving the branch without a manager for four weeks. Upon his return, a review of the marketing commitments to customers for the ongoing year was made. On the basis of being over budget, all agreements were cancelled. Customers became irate over commitments being cancelled well into the fiscal year. New policies developed to favor large customers were rejected by these customers as a matter of principle. With the buildup of interest and outrage surrounding the new manager, the change in marketing plans had a disastrous effect. The Washington area trade association for contractors wrote a letter critical of Neil Jones with the threat of boycotting purchase unless the situation changed. Related developments included the dismissal of one customer service representative and two salesmen taking medical disability.

Sam Parker continued to look at the Washington report. Sales were off almost 50 percent from quota. Since budgets were developed based on quota, the operation was losing considerable amounts of money. He knew that something was terribly wrong and must be rectified immediately.

QUESTIONS

1. What were the primary communication deficiencies in the Washington branch of the Climate Company?

2. While Neil Jones managed to create stress in the Washington branch, was it totally negative?

3. Assuming you were in Sam Parker's position, how would you deal with Neil Jones?

19

HOUSEHOLD AND HARDWARE PRODUCTS, INC.

It was a typical Wednesday afternoon in April when Hal Jordan, sales representative for Household and Hardware Products, Inc. (HHP), called his answering service for any important messages. Sherri, the manager's secretary, had called twice to tell Hal to contact his office immediately. He quickly called, thinking, "What could be the big deal this time?" Sherri informed him that he was to drive to the New Jersey office on Monday morning for a meeting and to pick up Pete Hamner on the way.

Pete is the sales representative in the Washington, D.C. area and is a good friend of Hal's. Pete and Hal had been with HHP four-and-a-half and five years respectively and had grown up in the job. Their present territories were the first assignments for each, and generally speaking, both had much in common including their boss, Tom Anders.

Tom Anders is a 54-year-old sales manager who has been with the company for 25 years and has held several sales positions during this period. Tom has 15 salesmen working for him, and he reports to Bill Jenson, vice-president of marketing for HHP.

Hal decided to call Pete that evening since Tom was out, to find out if he knew what this meeting was about. In the conversation, Pete indicated that all he knew was that Tom was displeased with the branch sales figures and probably had something he would attempt to do in order to rectify them. In the meantime, Hal had to spend the next two days trying to change his appointments, one of which he had just succeeded in getting after eight weeks of trying!

Monday morning arrived, with Hal leaving at 6 a.m. in order to make it to the New Jersey office by noon. As he drove north, he couldn't help thinking about the aggravation Tom had caused with his off-the-wall management. Of course Hal told himself that if Tom had more years with the company he could have retired; as it stands, he is stuck with him.

Hal picked Pete up and drove to the office, with Tom being the primary target of conversation. After lunch, the 15 salesmen and Tom filed into the conference room for the big meeting. It started something like this: "Guys, you are not getting the job done and we have to get you on track." He proceeded to use the overhead projector to display forecasted versus actual performance, paying attention to each individual's figures as he went down the list. After all were either chastised or praised, Tom laid out the objectives for the second quarter for each individual. At that point he asked for comments. Most of the personnel paid him lip service and reluctantly agreed to achieve the objectives and have game plans ready for the next day.

After a coffee break, the meeting resumed with a presentation of a new product program by Rick Backus, a salesman for the packaged abrasives product group. About 4 p.m. Tom returned to center stage to tie up the meeting with the consoling statement, "Gentlemen, what I'm giving you as far as grief is only half of what I'm getting from headquarters." At that point Hal decided to ask Tom if anything was being done to correct the problems with the merchandising plan, distribution center screw-ups, and general unsynchronized introductions of new products. Of course, this was all asked quite diplomatically in a lengthy question. Tom thought for a whole second and said, "I'm sure they are working on it. Well, fellas, let's call it a day. See you tomorrow. If you have any questions save them for your individual meetings."

Pete and Hal drove to their hotel, checked in, and then got together with the other salesmen who were staying over. As expected after a long browbeating like that one, the conversation turned to Tom's meeting. Hal said little, knowing full well that Tom's "ears," Bruce Jacobs, was in the group. Bruce is a real politician; if it helps him, he does it. After a couple of hours of beer and shop talk, everyone had dinner and retired for the evening.

The next day proceeded with private business reviews with Tom Anders. Two of the salesmen, Greg and Mike, had an 11 a.m. flight home, so Pete and Hal ended up third and fourth on the list. During the interim, they visited with their sales coordinators, cleaned out their files, checked on back-orders, and pleaded with the credit supervisors to "loosen up." Then they socialized until 10 a.m. when Tom sent for Hal.

After the typical pleasantries had been exchanged, Tom reviewed Hal's various accounts. When Hal pointed out a number of problems and potential problems, Tom did not propose any viable solutions. An example of this is demonstrated in the following conversation:

Tom: Hal, what seems to be your problem?

Hal: Well, Tom, HHP raised the price of bulk tape 15 percent last April followed by 19 percent in July and 13 percent in January of this year! We are out of the ballpark. I have lost my three largest customers, which represented big bucks to HHP.

Tom: Well, that's why we want to sell the packaged tape.

Hal: But the customer doesn't want $45,000 worth of packaged tape! I think we need to concentrate on what the customer wants and not what we want to sell. Also, we have discontinued our adhesives, which leaves me with $20,000 worth of history! How the hell am I supposed to be up by 17 percent over last year? I'm ahead of the branch average at 9.7 percent. Tom, I'm certainly not without fault, but realistically it's going to take time to make up the lost business.

Tom: Well, I think you ought to review your figures again. Nevertheless, our primary objective today is to determine the target for next quarter.

After further discussion, Tom wrote down some specific objectives, thanked Hal for his time, and excused him so the next salesman could have a review.

Because the next review was Pete's, Hal waited because Pete would be riding back with him. It was almost noon when Pete finally exited. After a quick lunch, they left on the trip back. The bulk of the conversation involved Tom, and more specifically, Tom's performance as sales manager.

Pete: You know, Hal, I don't think Tom has the faintest idea of what he is doing.

Hal: Tom is just hanging on to retire, and his objective is to outlast the pressure for figures. He says so many different things that it's hard to figure out what he is going to do next. I can honestly say that he has made some adjustment to his travel plans one week before every trip to my office in the last year. Half of the time he promises my customers things we can't deliver.

Pete: Last time Tom was down we called on my largest customer. While I was trying to discuss several of our programs, Tom got off on some tangent and got involved in trying to get a deal on dishes that his wife wanted for their new beach home. Here I was presenting this guy as my boss, a sales manager for HHP, and he acted like that! I really have trouble respecting him and taking him seriously when he tells me to do a better job.

Hal: I can really identify with that predicament. That has happened to me so often I couldn't count the times. On one hand, we are supposed to be concerned with professionalism (as evaluated on our performance review) and then he does everything to erase that image from the customer's mind. On the other hand, he can be great with the big customers when he puts his mind to it. In fact, with my largest customer, the ABC Co., the vice-president of sales rarely goes to lunch with representatives, but goes with Tom and me every trip. In plain English, it's just darn frustrating to have inconsistent directions given and then changed in the same breath.

Pete: Tom does little to teach us the job and motivate; I really have no way of knowing what he thinks of me unless he's landing into me. On the other hand, Tom does have some good points, especially his concern for us as people.

Hal: You're probably right. I do remember the time he let me have an extra day off to travel to be with my brother during his wedding weekend, but I guess that is what makes it so hard. He is a good, fair guy but a poor leader. The sad part is that every one of us has very little respect for him as a boss. Aside from work, Tom is an okay guy. What really irritates me is how he starts playing one of us against the other. What you do depends on you and the accounts you serve. Just because you have a particular company to sell $210,000 of energy products doesn't mean I can get one of my customers to do the same. They are different accounts with a whole different philosophy.

Pete: We have five good guys in this branch, but because Tom doesn't have it together, we are only managing to produce average performances as a group. I remember the time, I think it was October, he was sitting with me going through my trip file. "We need to discuss dealers," Tom said. However, last June he told me to work more closely with our distributors! Essentially, he just "wings it," and I am tired of it.

Hal: Pete, I guess we either have to get out or shut up until Tom retires.

The trip seemed to go quickly and they were at Pete's house before they knew it. As Hal headed home, he began to think of other, less drastic alternatives to this predicament. After all, he was working at night on a graduate degree, which the company was paying for. He did not want to miss out on this benefit. Resigning himself to the fact that he better keep his job, he began brainstorming to come up with some way of helping Tom to do a better job for all of the sales personnel.

QUESTIONS

1. Given the existing circumstances, what is the essential problem and what characteristics pertain to it?

2. What are the effects of Tom's leadership, as exemplified by the lack of respect given to him by the sales personnel?

20

CONTINENTAL CHEMICAL COMPANY, INC.

Soon after World War I, American industrial leaders sought ways to end the foreign domination of the chemical industry. This monopoly had resulted in drastic wartime shortages of dyes, pharmaceuticals, and other necessities that had long been supplied, for the most part, by German manufacturers. Motivated by the idea that a pooling of effort might give the United States a significant start toward strengthening domestic production, a group of men heading five chemical enterprises embarked on a joint venture.

Thus, in 1920, the Continental Chemical Company was formed by the consolidation of the Baker Company, supplying coal-tar chemicals; March Chemical Company, specializing in industrial acids; Eastern Chemical Company, a leading dye concern; Brace Solvent Company, manufacturing coke and its by-products; and Solvent Process Company, a manufacturer of alkalies and nitrogen materials. These five subsidiary companies became operating divisions of Continental Chemical: Baker and Eastern in 1941 and the others in 1947. This changeover to "divisions" was designed to strengthen corporate unity.

Traditionally a leading manufacturer of basic chemicals for industry, Continental has research and expansion programs that have not only strengthened its position as a basic supplier, but have also created a wealth of upgraded chemicals as well as some products that are available directly to retail purchasers.

From time to time, the corporation's divisional structure has been realigned to meet the needs of growing, more complex operations. A major reorganization took place in 1979 to rationalize manufacturing operations and consolidate product-line groupings, while simultaneously allowing major business areas to pursue policies most appropriate to their markets. Currently, manufacturing is carried on in six operating companies within the corporation: chemical; fibers and plastics; oil and gas; hospital and laboratory supplies; electrical products; automotive products; and other operations, including an automotive safety restraint group, several industrial products businesses, and one consumer products operation. Continental Chemical International directs export sales and manufacturing interests outside North America.

FIBERS AND PLASTICS COMPANY

The fibers and plastics company is located in Georgia and specializes in the production and marketing of Continental's Apollo nylon, which was initiated by the former Eastern Chemical Company after several decades of corporate research and pilot-plant study. The plant currently employs about 1,500 hourly workers represented by nine separate bargaining labor unions, and about 300 salaried supervisory and management personnel.

One of the key departments within the fibers and plastics plant is analytical services, which is responsible for the monitoring of quality parameters of production intermediates at various steps along the process. In addition, investigations of special projects are performed.

The department consists of about 65 employees, including 24 routine technicians, or eight per shift, on

a rotating, swing-shift schedule. These routine technicians perform the required analyses on raw materials,
intermediates, and finished product on a continuous,
24-hour operation. Seven of the eight technicians on
each shift are actually required to perform analyses;
the eighth person, who is designated chief technician,
is responsible for teletyping the results of the analyses
to the various areas of the plant and maintaining the
written logbooks. Additionally, the chief may also be
required to perform minor instrument repairs and to
contact a member of management if a situation arises
that requires a management decision.

In addition to these 24 routine technicians, there
are about 25 nonroutine technicians who all work the
daylight shift Monday through Friday (a preferred
shift). These technicians report directly to a chemist.
Nonroutine technicians are responsible for some of the
more complex, time-consuming analyses not done by
the routine group, as well as the special project work
assigned to them by their chemists. Both the routine
and nonroutine technicians are hourly workers who
are members of a chemical workers' union.

Supervising the work of the nonroutine technicians are six professional, college graduate chemists.
The chemists are salaried, first-line supervisors, and it
is an important part of their task to bridge the gap
between management and labor. They are assigned
projects by the chemical supervisors and must then
allocate the required duties among their assigned nonroutine technicians in an effective fashion.

There are three chemical supervisors and a foreman on the next level on the organizational hierarchy,
with each reporting to the manager of analytical services. Each supervisor has primary responsibility for
several key production areas, while the foreman is in
charge of scheduling the technicians' workweeks.

MARK NELSON, CHEMIST

Mark Nelson, a recent graduate in chemistry, was hired by Continental Chemical in 1981. He had three years experience in another industry prior to joining Continental, but had almost no direct supervisory experience. In spite of this fact, however, both the personnel manager and the manager of the analytical services department at the Georgia plant felt that Nelson would be a welcome injection of new blood into the laboratory organization.

Nelson's first assignment was in a chemist's position under Ken Knowles, a young chemical supervisor who had been with the organization for about 10 years. Ken was a personable fellow and easy to get along with, but he never passed up an opportunity to "lick his boss's boots," behavior that Nelson viewed with some contempt.

Nelson was promptly given two nonroutine technicians and a long list of unfinished projects that had been started by his predecessor. He did quite well, considering the circumstances, and quickly became well liked among all of the nonroutine technicians despite the management position he held. He was known as fair and friendly, and he rapidly established a reputation as an expert chemical problem-solver.

About 10 months after Nelson began working for Continental, a directive was issued by the department manager that required all six chemists to undergo job rotation; that is, all were switched to different groups, presumably to broaden plant experience and force the chemists to learn about different areas of operation.

Nelson's new assignment called for him to report to another chemical supervisor, Elmer Dixon. Dixon was a 35-year employee of Continental with responsibility for the quality control in two important areas of production: sulfuric acid and ammonium sulfate. A total of seven nonroutine technicians were assigned to tasks in these areas. Dixon did not have a great deal of respect for the hourly workers, and in fact considered them to be the lowest form of life there was. If they possessed any intelligence at all, they would be in management! He was a very nervous individual who lacked the ability to make even the most mundane decisions without first consulting his boss, the manager. Dixon was despised by all seven of his assigned technicians, who referred to him as "Oz" behind his back because his attempts to be tough and authoritative were merely a mask of the real Dixon. Dixon viewed the position of chemist merely as a glorified errand boy and messenger between him and his crew of technicians, since once a decision had been reached, he wanted it passed down in a very autocratic and intimidating manner. Dixon was also anachronistic, preferring the old way of wet-chemical analysis to the newer, more accurate methods in which Nelson was well versed.

Unwillingly thrust into this situation, Nelson once again demonstrated his ability to become well liked among his seven assignees, who despite being classified as "nonroutine technician" performed little more than boring, monotonous, routine work. The technicians only did what was required without ever performing above and beyond the call of duty.

Nelson, the young, relatively inexperienced rookie, was determined to increase the productivity in his group by motivating his people to perform. He had no authority to alter the monetary reward schedule, but he did have a few new ideas he felt would be worth a try, including rotating job assignments, modifying work-week scheduling, and conducting training sessions in newer, more modern analytical methods.

All of Nelson's proposed changes were resoundingly vetoed by Dixon, who was totally against changes of any sort, especially if he had not initiated them. Additionally, the technicians were generally against the changes as well. (Each one had been doing virtually the same identical job for over 25 years and were similarly threatened when changes were mentioned, since they had become comfortable with the present format of their jobs.)

After a year of working for Dixon, Nelson was given a performance review, in which Dixon wrote that Nelson was a "young, inexperienced man, full of radical ideas, bent on beating the system and rocking the boat. If he had devoted half of the time he spent in trying to change the status quo to doing what I told him to do, he'd have been an excellent employee. As it is, he's only been 'acceptable'."

After the performance review, Nelson felt defeated and saw that his creative efforts were effectively blocked at both ends of his only channel of expression. He became insolent, demotivated, and ceased trying to be creative and modernistic. Although he was neither happy nor satisfied, he became increasingly aware that all Dixon had wanted was a yes-man. Dixon then frequently commented to Nelson that he was glad Nelson had chosen to settle down and accept what he could not change.

Nelson, in only two short years, recognized that he could not become the kind of supervisor he wanted to be in the present system. He now had a personal dilemma: should he just plod along into obscurity and accept the fact that he was destined to be dissatisfied; should he request a transfer to another department or another plant; or should he give up altogether and seek another career outlet for his energies?

QUESTIONS

1. Why did Mark Nelson encounter so much difficulty in attempting to modernize the work effort in Dixon's group?

2. What is Nelson's "best" course of action, given the alternatives he has established for himself?

21

MAIN STREET CORPORATION: COMMERCIAL ACCOUNTS DIVISION

While Stan Evans is out of town on business, Carol Wingfield takes a call for him.

"Carol, this is Ben Carter. I'm calling from New York City because I'm so concerned that I couldn't wait until I got back in town. Nothing personal, but I really believe that your division's latest report misrepresents the facts. How can you say that our work is 'superficial'? I need to make an appointment to talk with Mr. Evans since the trend seems to be increased bias against my department."

Mr. Evans returns on Monday but works on a project that has top priority, so returns no phone calls. Still, he isn't too surprised when Ben Carter drops in at 4:30 p.m. For the next hour, Ben expresses his concern to the entire commercial accounts division (CAD), except Brian Jensen, who was out of town on business.

> In these economic times, more corporate borrowers than ever depend on collateral control systems that the collateral security department (CSD) provides, to obtain financing. CSD has made $3,000,000 in fees from our bank's customers this year but our own bank account officers don't recommend me after they read in CAD's report that our work is "superficial." I would prefer that you suggest specific remedies, rather than make blanket statements that imply that CSD isn't worth a damn. I realize that most of you are not that familiar with the work we do, but I've just returned from a conference of my peers in New York City and I assure you that our CSD program is the envy of the industry.

Larry Roberts confronted Ben with some specific problems that he had encountered in preparing CAD's reports, including: (1) total lack of information; (2) contradictory information; and (3) passing the buck for responsibility for the loans protected by CSD's control systems. Ben Carter replied at length.

Stan Evans assured Ben that he realized that starting a new department with limited personnel was difficult enough without unwarranted criticism, since he had been in the same position seven years ago. "We will certainly avoid the inflammatory word 'superficial' in the future and I'll continue to forward to you copies of reports pertaining to loans for which CSD controls collateral. That way you can contact us about any disagreements you might have."

Carol believed that Stan had smoothed over the conflict temporarily, but Larry told her that his opinion of CSD had not changed.

BACKGROUND

Stan Evans managed the commercial accounts division of Main Street Corporation, a statewide bank holding company. CAD reported administratively to the general auditor, who in turn reported to the board of directors. However, CAD was a staff function, obtaining information from the regional account officers and reporting on loan quality to the senior regional officers, the respective heads of commercial banking (Jeff Black), and operations. Any disagreement between the senior regional officers and CAD was arbitrated by Jeff Black's assistant.

No such clearcut grievance procedure was available to Ben Carter. His newly formed collateral security department (CSD) provided additional collateral control, which the bank generally required as a condition of lending to a weaker borrower. This service was previously purchased from national firms, of which there were only a few. Ben reported to Jeff Black, so he could be affected by any negative reports that Mr. Black received from CAD concerning loans which CSD also serviced. However, CSD and CAD had no direct ties.

FORMAL GROUP CONFLICT

The two groups had different subgoals, with CSD seeking to maximize sales of services and CAD seeking to minimize losses. This line/staff differentiation also existed between the senior regional officers and CAD, but their differences were usually over specific loans (which were to be resolved by the arbitrator) and not a general feeling of bias.

Both CAD and CSD were small and highly specialized groups. Carol knew very little about CSD operations so she was not able to judge the accuracy of Ben Carter's statement that his program was more conservative and complete than those of the national firms. The only CAD member familiar with CSD operations was Brian Jensen, who applied for the position of establishing/managing CSD and prepared a lengthy "white paper," which differed markedly in some respects from the policy and procedures developed by Ben Carter. Ben still referred to Brian Jensen as a doubter, so personalities could have been a cause of conflict.

CSD was new, and Ben felt that he was on trial. This attitude alone could account for some of the conflict as well as CAD personnel's tendency to be especially cautious about that with which they were unfamiliar. Three of the five CAD members had backgrounds in bank regulatory agencies so were trained to seek the exceptions to prudent banking practices.

One of Ben Carter's pet complaints was the inordinate amount of time he had to spend helping CAD personnel to obtain information. This scarce resource also affected CAD. Larry Roberts' complaints about lack of, and contradictory, information were inspired by the extra time that he had to spend clarifying these matters. Carol sympathized with Larry, because on a fact-finding tour at CSD, she had spent additional time sorting through three months' worth of information that had not been filed.

It appeared that horizontal communication between CSD and CAD and between CSD and the regional account officers was not working well. Conflict was not being resolved because there was no established method of expressing criticism, and no one was certain as to who was in charge of what!

CONFLICT RESOLUTION

In their discussion, Larry had demonstrated a desire to confront the major issues, whereas Stan attempted to smooth them over. Top management had already established a superordinate goal, since both CAD and CSD wanted the bank to be profitable. However, this did not draw the groups together because management had also charged each group with achieving this goal in a different way.

Stan Evans could have sent one or more of his subordinates to a seminar on CSD operations that was sponsored by a national banking group. This would have given CAD members a common background in order to communicate with Ben Carter, as well as a factual basis for judging his performance. However, Stan rejected this suggestion for budgetary reasons.

In the past, when one senior regional officer charged CAD with being overcritical, top management resolved the issue by redefining the scope of CAD's responsibilities. This compromise pleased the senior regional officer and relieved CAD of tiresome, petty problems in order to concentrate on essential deviations from policy.

Perhaps relations between the groups would stabilize once CSD was firmly established. Then Ben Carter could turn his attention from setting up procedures to controlling operations, and if necessary, request additional personnel to ease the load. If Ben had enough subordinates to file the three-month backlog and follow formal record-keeping procedures, CAD might not need to ask so many questions.

Top management could clarify some of the ambiguity over authority/responsibility for the loans by enforcing the stated policy that the "regional account officers are ultimately responsible for the quality of their loans." Ben Carter recently reminded the account officers of this with no noticeable response, so appealing to someone with authority over both CSD and the regional officers may be the only effective method of resolving this.

Perhaps this conflict between CAD and CSD was not entirely dysfunctional since it encouraged CAD to learn more about CSD operations and forced CSD to develop the best program possible in order to avoid criticism. If this were the case, it might be premature for top management to compromise the work of either group. Nevertheless, top management, especially Jeff Black, felt that some action was required because of the necessity for compatibility between the two groups. Jeff was not sure of the best approach to resolving the conflict and was even considering contacting a local management consultant for help.

QUESTIONS

1. A great deal of discussion generally centers on the dysfunctional aspects of conflict and ways to alleviate them. Are there any functional aspects to conflict?

2. Assume the role of an outside management consultant. What action would you recommend to Jeff Black regarding the conflict between CAD and CSD?

22

ALLSTAR FURNITURE COMPANY

Joe Davis sat in the lobby of Furniture City Bank, waiting for his appointment with Bill Adkins, vice-president of commercial lending. Six months ago, Joe borrowed $25,000 to finance the purchase of Starway Woodworking Company, a small furniture manufacturing operation, which he subsequently renamed Allstar Furniture Company. Although the company had been able to meet its first quarterly loan payment, it was now past due on the second, and the bank had requested that Joe come in and discuss the situation.

In addition to missing the loan payment, the company was behind on all of its accounts payable and could no longer purchase materials on credit. Several orders were sitting on the plant floor waiting for completion. Shipping delays were causing customers to take their orders elsewhere. The most pressing situation involved the company payroll account, which could fund only one more weekly payroll.

Joe wondered how the condition of the company could have gotten this bad in such a short period of time. He had a gut feeling that his production and financial problems were the direct result of "people" problems in the plant. Joe was anxious to talk to Bill Adkins, but he knew he would have to present a specific strategy for remedying the situation before the bank would be willing to provide the financial assistance. As he waited, Joe began to recall the events of the past six months.

BACKGROUND

The company Joe purchased, Starway Woodworking, had been in business for 10 years in High Point, North Carolina, an area recognized as a leading furniture manufacturing city. Even though Starway specialized in lower quality furniture frames, it had been a successful business due largely to the efforts of its owner, Buck Johnson. Buck had been in furniture manufacturing all of his life and knew what it took to run a shop on a day-to-day basis.

Buck had an interesting relationship with his employees. During working hours he provided constant guidance and expected his employees to put forth a high level of effort, which they usually did. When the workday ended, however, he tended to look the other way when his employees frequently drank to excess. In fact, Buck had been known to have a few drinks with his employees, and felt that what they did on their off time was their business.

In August 1981, Buck suffered a heart attack and was forced into semiretirement. Although he hoped to return to the shop on a part-time basis, it was clear that he would not be able to devote the effort that he had previously given the company. As a result, Starway was offered for sale, and Buck notified his employees. His most loyal employees agreed to stay on until the company was sold and clean up any unfinished business.

Joe Davis immediately recognized Starway as an excellent investment opportunity. His position as a vice-president of a large furniture company afforded him a comfortable living, but for the past few years he had toyed with the idea of starting up a small family business. After visiting Starway, Joe reached an agreement with Buck Johnson to purchase the company for

$25,000. The conditions of the sale included the retention of any previous employees who wished to stay on and offering employment to Buck, in a supervisory position. Joe felt this was an ideal arrangement since his son and son-in-law were eventually going to manage the business but neither had enough experience to run the plant initially.

Next, Joe had to arrange the financing. After an initial meeting with Bill Adkins, Joe was asked to prepare a loan proposal for the bank's consideration as well as an overall business plan for the company. The basic elements of the plan were as follows:

1. Starway Manufacturing would be renamed All-star Furniture Company, Incorporated, with Joe Davis holding the stock.

2. Joe Davis would provide the overall management of the company, although he was going to keep his present job and only visit the new company as needed.

3. Greg Davis and Jeff Howard (Joe's son and son-in-law) would provide the day-to-day management of the company, assisted, at least initially, by Buck Johnson, the previous owner.

4. Initial emphasis would be placed on continuing with existing low quality business, but the eventual goal was to ease out of this market into higher quality business. This transition would require skills not presently available in the existing staff.

After reviewing the business plan and the projected financial statements, Bill Adkins agreed that on paper the venture looked good. He was troubled, however, with the proposed management structure. Neither Greg Davis nor Jeff Howard had any direct experience in managing a plant, and with Joe remaining in his present position, the initial success of the company appeared to hinge on Buck Johnson. When Bill voiced his concerns, Joe revealed that he was not totally satisfied in his permanent job and would most likely resign in the near future to work full time at Allstar. The loan was eventually approved, although the bank required that Joe place a second mortgage on his home, in addition to pledging the plant's equipment as collateral.

THE NEW LEADERSHIP

Allstar Furniture was incorporated on November 1, 1981. The following Monday, Joe scheduled a meeting for all employees. Also in attendance were Buck Johnson, Greg Davis, and Jeff Howard. During the meeting Jeff conveyed the following message:

> Most of you are aware that I am the new owner of this company. You probably have some apprehension about what changes may be in store. First, let me say that each of you can continue to work here if you so desire. Although Buck is not back to 100 percent yet, he will be assisting me on a part-time basis, and I would expect things to run pretty much the same as in the past.
>
> I also want to introduce my son, Greg Davis, and my son-in-law, Jeff Howard. They will also be assisting me in running the plant.
>
> As for myself, I will be visiting the plant periodically to monitor our progress. All I ask is that you continue to do your jobs and help us make this transition period as smooth as possible.

When the meeting concluded, the employees all agreed to stay on with the company. Most of them were somewhat relieved that there would be no drastic changes and were quite impressed with Joe Davis.

During the next two months, several new accounts were opened and production increased to the point where additional factory workers were hired. Buck was working every morning, and things were running smoothly. Greg and Jeff were spending their time in the various departments, trying to get an overview of the entire operation. Greg had finished one year of college and tended to spend most of his time in the machine room, assembly, and shipping/receiving. Jeff, who had a college degree in business, leaned more toward sales, inventory control, and administration.

In early January, Buck's health declined to the point where he was placed back in the hospital for an extended period. At the same time, Allstar landed two new "high-end" accounts. These new orders required high levels of skill and craftsmanship to complete. To gear up for this production, an order was made for a substantial quantity of high quality raw materials, such as prime maple and walnut stock. Several of the employees began to feel uneasy when these materials were delivered. Many had only worked with the lower quality materials Buck had used and had no real experience in making these high quality pieces. Complicating the situation was the fact that Joe Davis had become extremely busy in his permanent job and was traveling quite a bit. As a result, he was able to visit the plant only rarely.

During the next three months things deteriorated rapidly. A high degree of tension developed in the plant due to the time and quality pressures placed on the employees by the new orders. Overall, a negative attitude toward the high quality work became evident.

Jeff overheard the following comments between Eddie and Ron, who had been two of Buck's best employees.

Eddie: I'm getting fed up with this place. This morning Greg jumped on my case because I messed up a pair of walnut chair legs. I told him before I started that I didn't know how to sand walnut.

Ron: I know how you feel. Why do we have to make this hard stuff anyway? Buck always made out OK selling the cheap frames, and there wasn't any pressure. I think Jeff is trying to sell accounts that are over our head.

This low morale led to more serious problems. Some of the workers were coming in with hangovers, and it was affecting their work. Others were not coming in at all. Several oldtimers quit. The tension in the plant seemed to peak a month ago, when Jeff confronted Eddie about his drinking and asked him to go home until he was sober enough to work. Eddie responded by quitting. The following remarks are representative of his comments:

> Ever since Buck got sick again, things have been bad. When he was here we had someone who we could go to with our problems. He knew how to do things right. Now we don't even know who our boss is. Mr. Davis is never here, and no one has shown us how to make those walnut chairs. We are all drinking more now because there's so much pressure on us. Besides, Buck never came down on us for drinking.

During these few months, production suffered drastically and financial problems grew. Greg and Jeff tried to manage the business as well as they could, but there was a growing conflict, even between them, since they were unsure of their exact responsibilities. On several occasions they had disagreed on important decisions. This conflict tended to distort the information that was passed along to Joe, which made it difficult for him to know exactly what was going on at the plant.

Now Joe is in financial trouble and needs a recovery plan. He is sure that Bill Adkins will want evidence that the business can still be successful. What changes can Joe make to support this?

QUESTIONS

1. What are the various symptoms that suggest a problem exists at Allstar?

2. What are the major problems that exist within the current framework of Allstar?

3. How could Joe Davis have avoided these problems? What are his existing alternative courses of action?

23

DIVERSIFIED PRODUCTS CORPORATION

After being hired two-and-a-half years ago as an intermediate accountant by Diversified Products Corporation, Joe Arnold was evaluating his status and career development opportunities within the corporate accounting and consolidation department of Diversified. From the outset Joe had expressed a strong desire to learn all phases of the corporate finance, accounting, and control functions. He felt that gaining experience in these areas would aid the company in the long run while providing him an initial broad-based operational understanding from which to work. However, Joe's supervisor, Mr. Willison, indicated on several occasions that there was little turnover in the group, and no lateral transfer or promotional opportunities appeared likely in the near future. Willison added that Arnold was being paid a more than equitable salary and was expected to perform the specific duties of his job with competence. As he often pointed out, "if you continue to do a good job and get enough experience at it, the chance to move up will come. Don't concern yourself with the other functions. If everyone does his individual job well, then as a group we'll move forward. Look at me. I've worked in the consolidation department for 14 years and realize that it has been a worthwhile experience concentrating in this area."

COMPANY BACKGROUND

Diversified Products Corporation is a major multinational manufacturer and is among the world's largest vertically integrated companies. Headquartered in Virginia, Diversified can be segmented into three generic business groups: energy, technology, and paper. All of these units were encouraged to operate in a decentralized manner within the parent company, since 90 percent of these businesses had been acquired. Each group had its own vice-president and five divisions separately headed by a general manager, and were organized departmentally by product. With regard to the finance, accounting, and control functions, each group had a controller with inventory, financial reporting, fixed asset, accounts payable, and billing department responsibility. All of this information at the group level was monitored in terms of reporting procedures by corporate finance, accounting, and control. Corporate finance, among its many other responsibilities, reported company share earnings to the financial publics, issued quarterly company financial reports to the executive committee, published Diversified's annual report, and controlled group operating levels.

FINANCE, ACCOUNTING, AND CONTROL

Diversified Product Corporation's finance, accounting, and control function was headed by the company's corporate controller, Mr. Raley, who reported to the executive vice-president and chief financial officer, Mr. Patton. Mr. Raley was a CPA and Mr. Patton, a lawyer. Together these two men spent their entire careers dedicating 66 years of combined service to Diversified and rose through the ranks to their current executive level positions. In his position, Patton was viewed as having a wide span of control over much of the company's staff functions (treasury, public relations, employee relations, controller) spreading himself too thin, but keeping a definite hand in all activities. Not known for developing strong managers under him, Patton kept the decision making at the highest level and made a policy of having his chain of command report on all major decisions.

Reporting to Mr. Raley were two directors: Mr. Anthony, control, and Mr. Lofton, reporting. More than anything else, these positions were designated as stepping stones to the position of controller and had responsibility for all departments. Such was the case with the current controller, Raley, and one previous incumbent, Jack Wheeling, who left the company after 23 years of service. Many believe Wheeling's departure was a result of conflicting views with Patton on several issues. This move enabled Raley, a person seen as maintaining similar ideals as Patton, to become controller. Furthermore, it was generally accepted throughout the organization that Mr. Lofton would be the likely successor to the position of controller once Patton retired in several years. Besides maintaining high status in the department, Mr. Lofton was viewed by subordinates as doing everything by the book. "My door is always open. If you have a problem, I can think of no better way to solve it than by good old fashioned face-to-face employee relations."

Over the years, when "intermediate" positions (two years experience) within the corporate finance, accounting, and control department became available, Diversified would generally go to the outside rather than transfer individuals from one of the operating groups or any of the other corporate financial reporting, tax, inventory, accounts payable, or fixed asset departments. Management's thinking was generally that people in these groups either did not meet the minimum qualifications of having a CPA or were overqualified, having been with the company for more than two years. "We like to grow our own, train them in the department's approach to doing things. Furthermore, they could have a biased view of procedural operations, coming from those groups."

Throughout the organization, hiring practices were conducted on a decentralized basis within each group. Manager's attitude was hands-off when other managers or the personnel office raised the possibility of an employee's availability for transfer to a particular accounting group to fill an existing opening at corporate or another operating unit. This conflict was most prevalent when managers had a high performer and would emphatically refuse to part with the person. A typical response was, "If I allow one of my good people to leave my group to fill another opening, then I have to hire someone who has the same experience to fill that job, not to mention the time it will take to train a new person. It only moves the 'hole' in the organization somewhere else." Given this norm throughout the organization, when openings occurred and managers would volunteer an individual for transfer, the hiring manager would recognize that person as a below average employee and not consider him or her!

GROWTH AND DEVELOPMENT OPPORTUNITIES

Joe Arnold, CPA and BS in Accounting, was hired by Mr. Willison into the corporate accounting and consolidation department after Joe worked on Diversified's audit with a big eight accounting firm. While a member of the audit staff, Joe spent tireless hours of overtime, always asking insightful questions about how certain numbers were derived. He had an extremely professional approach in dealing with the company staff, yet demonstrated persistence in his own way when pursuing needed information.

During the last two-and-a-half years, Diversified had hired six individuals with similar education and experience to work as intermediate accountants in each of their corporate departments (Steven Jones, fixed assets; Tim Adams, accounts payable; Sheila Rhoads, inventories; Dan Barr, tax; and Diane Case, financial reporting). During this time most of these individuals participated in numerous personal development activities ranging from attending local seminars at a nearby university to continuing their education in an advanced degree program. Just recently Joe Arnold completed his MBA degree on a part-time basis through Diversified's tuition reimbursement program. "I feel like the MBA has given me a broad understanding not only of the interrelation of the accounting and financial departments, but also how each function fits into the overall operation of the company."

Performance appraisal time at Diversified primarily meant a brief meeting to present an individual's salary increase for the next year. However, during this year's review, Joe Arnold felt the need to probe several issues with Mr. Willison that seemed of great personal importance.

Telephone rings

Joe Arnold: Joe Arnold.

Mr. Willison: Joe, please come down to my office. It's salary time again.

Joe: Yes sir, on my way.

(Joe knocks on Mr. Willison's door)

Mr. Willison: Come right in, Joe, and have a seat. We won't be but a few minutes.

Joe: Yes, you mentioned on the phone that it was time for our department's annual reviews.

Mr. Willison: That's right, Joe, and I want to let you know what your salary increase for next year will be, since it has to be in by Friday to the payroll department *(hands Joe a piece of paper with the amount of increase written on it).* This will be reflected in your next paycheck.

Joe: *(Looks at piece of paper.)*

Mr. Willison: Well, are you satisfied?

Joe: $210 a month is probably an adequate increase, but compared to what standard, Mr. Willison? Am I an average, above average, or below average performer?

Mr. Willison: Joe, you are doing a fine job. Consider that good unless we indicate otherwise.

Joe: Mr. Willison, I've mentioned before that I believe it would be valuable to my career development at this early stage to be exposed to, and learn something about, the other finance, accounting, and control functions at corporate, possibly spending some time in each. My goal someday is to be a controller or in a treasurer's position, and it seems appropriate that to get to that level, one would need to know about all functions.

Mr. Willison: Joe, I don't see any transfer opportunities being available in the near future. I can only speak from experience. If you continue to perform your specific job duties, that is all we ask. Furthermore, we pay you well and provided tuition reimbursement for your MBA degree. Diversified is a great place to work, with good people who understand the years of experience it takes to move up in an organization. All we expect is good performance in return. Thank you, Joe. Have a good day.

Returning to his office, Joe considered his recent meeting with Mr. Willison and his time with Diversified over the past two-and-a-half years and how all this related to him personally.

QUESTIONS

1. How might the behavioral orientation of Joe Arnold and his peers differ from upper management's?

2. What motivates Joe at this particular point in his career? Is he being motivated through Willison's leadership?

3. If you were Joe, how would you react to Willison's assessment of your growth opportunities at Diversified? What action could you take in order to remedy the situation?

24

SPARKLE ALUMINUM COMPANY: HOME PRODUCTS DIVISION

John Olsen, vice-president of the home products division of Sparkle Aluminum Company, was reviewing the information gathered by a corporate team he had sent to his major plant, the Beckville Home Products Plant. John believed that the plant personnel had not been operating as an effective group. This belief was based on customer and sales department complaints concerning the meeting of deadlines and quality requirements. John had also received comments from several visitors to the plant that some intergroup conflicts were in evidence. Also, many vital developmental projects were behind schedule. When he asked Al Milton, the Beckville plant manager, about the allegations, John had not received a satisfactory answer. He therefore sent in a fact-finding team to gather information.

COMPANY HISTORY

The Sparkle Aluminum Company (SAC) is one of the largest manufacturers of aluminum and aluminum products in the country. The company had entered the home building products market once before in its corporate life. That entry into the market had been unsuccessful, and the company had withdrawn after suffering a considerable loss. This highly competitive market requires very little capital for a small businessman to enter. A small firm can easily buy aluminum and glass to build windows and doors. For just a little more initial capital, that firm can also buy machines to form aluminum siding, siding accessories, gutters, and downspouts.

Since a small business does not have to meet all the stringent government regulations, it has an immediate advantage. Also, a small business can usually avoid unions, and therefore it has a lower cost of labor. Since a small firm does not also manufacture the raw aluminum, it can usually have someone else stock this material and therefore eliminate stocking costs. However, because the home building market is the largest market for aluminum, seven years ago the company decided to again enter this field. SAC had used a step-child approach before of making the home market a part of an existing division. This time it decided to form a separate division, the home products division, to make the new entry. The division rapidly built five new facilities, with the largest being the Beckville plant.

The division had carved out a respectable market share, but only because it often gave discounts below stated wholesale prices to larger customers. Even though it had broken even at division level the previous year, it had lost money when corporate overhead was included. The division was under increasing pressure to improve its profit situation.

PLANT HISTORY AND ORGANIZATION

Beckville is a very small farming community with a population of 1500. Most of the plant's production workers are either part-time or ex-farmers who live in or near Beckville or its larger neighbor, Culver. Culver is ten miles farther southeast and has a population of 8500.

Al Milton is the third plant manager at Beckville in the plant's six years of operation. The first manager had formerly run his own building products manufacturing operation. He was released from Beckville because he did not fit into a large corporation's requirements. The second manager was also hired outside the company on the basis of his building products experience. He resigned after two years, citing excessive job pressure and resulting ill health as reasons for leaving.

The plant had made money the previous year based on a standard cost system in force in the plant. However, this system included a volume variance allowance, which made the plant look better than it actually was. It took into account that the volume of the plant was less than its capability due to lower than normal sales by the sales group. Therefore, the plant was also under constant pressure to cut costs so that the division could show an overall profitable situation.

The Beckville plant employs about 430 people consisting of 100 salaried employees, with the remainder comprised of members of the Steelworkers Union. The following is a description of the department heads and other key personnel directly involved in the plant's daily operations.

Plant Manager: Al Milton is 49 years old and has been with SAC for 20 years. He has an engineering degree and has spent most of his career in sales with the Rolling Mill Division. He has been at the Beckville plant for four years. Before becoming plant manager two years ago, he was in charge of both the customer service and traffic and warehouse departments. He is known as a "workaholic," is divorced, and lives alone in an apartment in Beckville.

Production Superintendent: Richard Brown is 41 years old and never attended college. He grew up in the roughest streets of Cleveland and worked for Beckville's first plant manager before both came to work for SAC.

He started as the department superintendent over the siding department and siding paint line. He became good friends with Al Milton before Al became plant manager. Al made Richard production superintendent a year and a half ago.

Plant Engineer: Carl Slade is 29 years old and was asked to transfer to his present job only six months ago. After graduating from college with high honors in engineering, he worked at SAC's largest and best-run smelting plant. Though he has been out of school only seven years, he came to Beckville experienced in engineering, maintenance, and the running of these functions. He had been responsible for managing crews of up to 40 workers in his previous assignment. He was interviewed by Beckville's management and by the division's corporate staff before being asked to take the job.

Personnel Manager: Ben Olsen is 34 years old, married, and has two children. He transferred from another SAC plant three years ago and has been with SAC nine years.

Purchasing Manager: Rick Zeigler is 39 years old, married, and has three children. He is an experienced purchasing manager, and he came from the same plant as Ben Olsen two years ago. He bought a small farm just outside of Culver so that his family could transfer their three horses.

Siding Superintendent: Bill Newly grew up locally and started at Beckville the day the plant opened. He has never had college training, but he demonstrates an ability to deal with the local crews in the plant. He was made foreman a year after the plant was opened and was promoted to superintendent when Richard Brown was promoted to production superintendent.

Window and Door Superintendent: Larry Hill is 42 years old and a local product with no college training. He is known as somewhat of an introvert and was a tough foreman before taking over the department on a temporary basis almost nine months ago. His predecessor left to go into business for himself, and a suitable replacement has not been found.

Extrusion Superintendent: Harry Peale is 54 years old and has been in the extrusion business all his life.* The extrusion business "experts" are considered vagabonds, and Harry is no exception. He worked for SAC twice earlier before leaving for greener pastures. He has been at Beckville for three-and-one-half years, an average length of stay in one place for Harry. His tendency toward "backbiting" is as well known as his extrusion expertise.

Maintenance Superintendent: Ned Hardy is 43 years old. He started his career as a journeyman machinist and is very experienced in maintenance. He is a by-the-book individual and runs a tight operation. He takes a hard line with the various department heads when he feels damage to machinery is user-inflicted.

THE CORPORATE INVESTIGATION TEAM

The corporate team put together by the vice-president was headed by the corporate personnel manager. Members on the team included representatives from corporate industrial engineering, finance, design engineering, and quality control. The team spent one week at Beckville during which time they attended staff meet-

---

*An extrusion press is a device that takes a cylindrical tube of heated aluminum or other soft metal and pushes it through a die to make a special shape. The process can be likened to pushing on the sides of a tube of toothpaste to "extrude" the material inside.

ings, had private interviews with all department heads, and had informal conversations with people throughout the plant. The team also spent considerable time going over plant cost, production, scrap, turnover, returns, quality, and other records.

As a result of the intense, week-long investigation, there appeared to be several areas of concern to SAC. Specifically, the team members found the two staff meetings they attended to be somewhat subdued. They attributed this fact to their presence, since they were told privately that the staff meetings were often very vocal and even hostile. The meetings usually included the plant manager, the production superintendent, the plant engineer, the purchasing, quality control, personnel, accounting, production control managers, the chief industrial engineer, and others depending on the subject. The chief industrial engineer was included in the meetings because a subject often arising in the meetings was the standard cost system. The preoccupation with this system was caused by the heavy stress put on it as a benchmark by which all departments and individuals were judged. Much interdepartmental quarreling involved who would be charged for what items and when under the system.

The team of investigators also found that, during the meetings, Al Milton left several times to accept phone calls from sales personnel with complaints or problems. Such calls seemed to disrupt the flow of the meetings and slowed down their progress.

A review of plant records indicated that scrap and returns were higher than a level that corporate headquarters considered acceptable. The records also indicated that a number of projects designed to alleviate such problems were running far behind schedule.

The interviews with department heads indicated a serious lack of consensus regarding the nature of the problem(s) that necessitated a visit from headquarters in the first place. For example, Al Milton stated that he felt that most of the plant problems would disappear if the sales department would sell enough products to load the plant. He believed that the intergroup problems were only a result of the pressure caused by the volume variance problem. On the other hand, Ben Olsen was concerned about the next negotiations with the union. He believed the plant would have to give the union a large increase, and this would worsen the situation compared to nonunion competitors.

Richard Brown (production superintendent) had the most to say of anyone interviewed, with the possible exception of Ned Hardy. Richard blamed the cost system, the maintenance department, and the sales department for the plant's problems. He also blamed the lack of a new window design, one of the major plant objectives and a major cause of window returns, on the corporate product design group. That group had been involved in this product because of its warranty and product liability considerations.

Richard also complained about the "car pool" making decisions for the plant without consulting him or Milton. The car pool consisted of several of the management team who lived outside of Beckville and who rode together to the plant. Ben Olsen, Carl Slade, Steve Kellogg, the chief industrial engineer and the assistant purchasing agent were all members of that group. Even one or two comments were made by foremen in the plant that the car pool ran the plant, not Al Milton.

In his interview, Carl Slade (plant engineer) did not have much to say to the team, except to question the whole idea of having corporate members make such an investigation. He wondered out loud that maybe such a method could even make matters worse. He did, however, say that he felt the plant was so busy putting out daily fires that nobody was allowed time to develop better systems or to do any real project work.

He said that his engineering crew ended up being highly paid technicians rather than engineers.

When he was given an opportunity to interview with the investigation team, Bill Newly (siding superintendent) complained about the raw material he received and the standards set for his workers. In addition, he complained that Richard Brown talked down to him and his people. He felt that his people deserved more respect for the good job they were doing. He also said that Al Milton was so involved in every detail of the plant's operation that he did not have time to discuss some ideas that Bill knew would reduce costs. But Bill also said that you have to respect someone like Al who was so dedicated that you were likely to see him at the plant at all hours of the day or night. Bill stated that he didn't always get along with Ned Hardy, but he did appreciate how Carl Slade had come into the plant in the middle of the night to solve operational problems when the maintenance department could not do so.

The other key interviewee during the team's investigation was Ned Hardy (maintenance superintendent). Ned initially pointed out that the maintenance and engineering departments were so understaffed that he was amazed they were even able to keep the plant going. He indicated that Carl Slade supported him in trying to institute a preventive maintenance program, but he said that Al Milton kept the department so tied up on petty emergencies that no time was available for developing such a program. He noted that two weeks earlier Al Milton had instructed two of his people to tear down a gutter machine when the machine had just been completely overhauled. A salesman had complained about some faulty product in the field that was later discovered to have been manufactured some six months earlier (before the last overhaul)!

The comments made by other workers in the plant varied greatly. One worker stated that management was changed so often that all you had to do was wait five minutes and a new set of directives would be out. Another stated that "pounds out the door" was all that interested management. A discussion with the plant nurse indicated that stress was a common malady in the plant. She was particularly concerned about Al Milton, who, she said, did not take care of himself.

Although the team was only asked to collect data and was not asked to make specific recommendations concerning the situation, they concluded their report by saying that they believed their investigation had shown that the appearance of intergroup conflict had a sound basis. They were particularly concerned with the undercurrent of tension they felt throughout the plant.

The team confirmed John Olsen's worst fears about the plant, but the report also brought up some other questions that involved the investigation itself. Now John had to decide what to do to get the plant back on the right track.

QUESTIONS

1. Was the fact-gathering method chosen by the vice-president effective?

2. What factors appear to be creating a lack of management group effectiveness in the Beckville plant?

3. What action should the vice-president take to try to improve the situation?

25

MORGAN SOUP COMPANY

After three months on the job, Beverly Jackson was much less excited with her position as staff accountant than she had anticipated. Working for a big company with a big salary had turned out to be a big letdown.

She wasn't alone in her perspective. During the past 12 months, the cost accounting department of the Morgan Soup Company had lost over 40 percent of its staff accountants in turnover. Beverly had observed that most of those who remained were as unhappy as she was with the lack of training and amount of overtime they had to work.

COMPANY HISTORY

Founded in 1925, the Morgan Soup Company has grown from a small-scale operation into one of the largest soup companies in the country. While the size of the market has only grown in proportion to the growth in the population, Morgan has been able to experience growth in sales and profits because of an excellent market strategy and well-placed advertising. The majority of the growth has been experienced in the last 15 years (1967–1982), and Morgan has expanded to meet the demand through the construction of new plant facilities. Morgan has also become an important force in the international food market.

COMPANY OPERATIONS

The manufacturing and packaging of the product is a fairly complex process that involves significant capital investment in plant and machinery as well as variable labor and material expense. There are over 500 different brand codes for Morgan's soups. While there are only 30 major varieties of soups, the packaging may vary significantly (individual servings, 10 oz., 18 oz. sizes); each packaging differentiation merits a separate brand code. Additionally, for exported soups, packaging must be changed to read in the appropriate language.

A brief explanation of the manufacturing process follows:

1. Direct materials for the manufacturing process are received daily and stored at the central warehouse until needed in operation.

2. The 30 varieties of soups are processed at the processing plant locations, which run 24 hours a day for seven days a week. There are five processing plant facilities that have from five to eight processing departments.

3. The products (liquid and solid components) are piped to the packaging facilities, which are located adjacent to each processing plant.

4. The packaging machinery is set up in units called "modules" by soup variety/brand to be containerized. The packaging plants operate on the same schedule as the processing plants.

5. The packaged goods are carried by conveyer belt to the finished goods warehouse to be stored until sold.

THE COST ACCOUNTING DEPARTMENT

The cost accounting department of Morgan is responsible for reporting monthly manufacturing results to executive management. The executives depend heavily on this information to isolate high-cost areas and possible budget overruns that may have an adverse effect on profits for the quarter. The timeliness and accuracy of the information is crucial to the decision-making process of Morgan's top management.

The organizational chart for the cost accounting department is shown in Figure 25.1. Reporting directly to the manager are two assistant managers—one for processing plant locations and one for packaging plants. Five supervisors report to the assistant managers, and each supervisor has six to eight accountants.

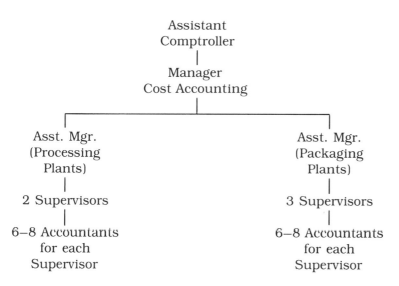

FIGURE 25.1 Cost accounting department organization

There are seven clerical/secretarial positions in the department for a total staff of 53. There are three potential levels for the staff accountants: junior accountant, senior accountant, and analyst.

The level of turnover within the cost accounting department has been a major concern as evidenced in a recent conversation between Bob Gaines, cost manager, and Harvey Johnson, assistant comptroller.

Harvey: Bob, with the salaries we offer accountants, I just can't understand why the turnover rate in your department is so high. It seems that since we have the best benefit package of any employer in the area and are in the top 10 percent in salaries, we'd have no trouble attracting and keeping qualified personnel. Considering the training period is about six months, the continual turnover in personnel is costing the company severely.

Bob: With the deadlines we operate under, and the close scrutiny our work receives, it is imperative that we recruit and maintain qualified people so that our overtime can be kept at a reasonable level.

Harvey: Yes, that's another thing. Your department ran $5,200 over budget last quarter in overtime.

Adding to the problems of training and turnover, the type of information furnished by the cost accounting department is detailed and technically demanding. As Morgan's growth has escalated over the past 10 years, systems development has not been able to keep pace. As a result, a lot of accounting work that could be computerized is still being done manually—adding to an already exorbitant overtime situation.

In addition, as Morgan's executive structure has grown, the demand for new and more sophisticated reporting has increased. The time constraints have

precluded the adequate documentation of job procedures. Most of the job knowledge is concentrated in
the personnel who have years of experience on the staff
(supervision and management). As a result, these individuals spend an inordinate part of what should be
management time on explaining how to calculate and
report manufacturing results accurately. There is no
contact between the manager and the accountant levels. While supervisors are involved in the day-to-day
activity with the staff accountants, some groups are
too large to allow for immediate response to all technical questions.

Due to the situation in such a critical area of control as the cost accounting department, the company's
comptroller decided that it would be beneficial to hire
an outside consulting firm for evaluative purposes.
Management Evaluation Services, Inc. was subsequently hired to conduct a department-wide survey in
order to isolate the key problem areas.

THE STUDY

The cost accounting staff was informed that during the
next two months, management consultants from Management Evaluation Services (MES) would be conducting interviews with each employee. They were informed
that the purpose of the interviews was to provide an
opportunity to express their attitudes toward the company in general and their own department in
particular.

After Beverly Jackson heard about the visit, she
became quite excited. She would finally have an opportunity to vent her frustrations! When it was time for
her interview, the conversation went as follows:

MES: We have a few questions concerning your employer. Please answer them as honestly as possible. All responses will be kept anonymous. The first concern we want to address is how well you feel your skills are utilized working at Morgan.

Beverly: In some ways, I feel that my skills are over-utilized—like having to work overtime constantly—but then some of the work that the accountants do is almost clerical, which takes much less skill. That's kind of a hard question to answer.

MES: I see. How do you feel about the training you've been given at Morgan? Has it prepared you for your workload?

Beverly: Not at all. Allan, my supervisor, does what he can, but things are always so hectic that he really doesn't have the time to do very much preparatory training. It's sort of a sink or swim situation.

MES: Well, how do you feel the rest of the management in the cost accounting department feels about you and your success at Morgan?

Beverly: I have no way of knowing. The only time I talked with them was when I interviewed at Morgan four months ago.

MES: Do you feel there is a chance for you to be promoted at Morgan, or do you feel that you will have to go elsewhere to reach the level to which you aspire?

Beverly: At this point, I plan to stay at least another year to find out if things will improve. I'm satisfied with my salary and the company's benefits couldn't be better. With all the turnover, something will probably happen to increase promotional opportunities.

MES: Getting back to Allan—do you feel that you
know what he expects of you in your job? Are communication channels open?

Question	Percent Agreeing
1. The physical surroundings where I carry out my work are satisfactory.	85%
2. I feel that I am paid a commensurate amount for the work I do.	90%
3. I feel that I have the freedom needed to operate in the most effective manner.	80%
4. I receive all the relevant information I need to carry out my job responsibilities.	70%
5. The training I have been given on the job is satisfactory.	40%
6. The company has excellent benefits for its employees.	100%
7. I have been afforded ample opportunity for promotion within the company.	20%
8. I know where I stand with my immediate supervisor.	40%
9. I know what is expected of me in my job.	50%
10. I believe the company is doing all it can to help me develop in my job.	50%
11. I think that my department management is genuinely interested in employees in the department and sees them as individuals rather than as machines to do work.	60%
12. I am encouraged about the way things are going in my department.	30%

FIGURE 25.2   Management Evaluation Services, Inc.
survey results

Beverly: To a degree, they are. I think the main problem about not knowing what to expect comes from the fact that there are no job procedures for any of the accounting jobs. If I just had some guidelines, I wouldn't have to depend on Allan as much. There would probably also be fewer mistakes if we had more documentation of job functions.

At the conclusion of the interviews, the consultants analyzed their findings and forwarded a report to the comptroller. (An overview of the findings is presented in Figure 25.2.) Although he was glad to have an outsider's assessment of the situation, the comptroller was not particularly pleased at some of the items in the report. He now felt that it was time to have a very serious meeting with the assistant comptroller and department manager to decide on the appropriate course(s) of action. The meeting was set for the following week.

QUESTIONS

1. What would you consider the three most significant problems facing cost accounting management?

2. What style of leadership do you feel would be the most effective in the cost accounting environment?

3. If you were the assistant comptroller, how would you handle the problem in cost accounting? Is a new manager the answer?

26

FIRST UNITED
NATIONAL BANK

First United National Bank, founded in 1919, is a statewide bank with 100 branch offices serving a population of approximately five million in its primary market areas. The smallest of Connecticut's 300-plus banks when founded, First United is now among the state's largest banks and ranks among the top 150 banking institutions in the country with assets approaching $4 billion and over 2,500 full-time employees.

Increased regulatory and market changes have significantly altered the complexion of the banking industry over the last decade. Three major changes affecting the industry are:

1. *Competition*—savings and loans, credit unions, and even brokerage houses are virtually becoming "banks" in terms of the services they offer.

2. *Consumer*—The consumer is becoming increasingly aware of banking alternatives.

3. *Costs*—There is increased pressure on profits due to increased costs of deposits (as a result of the gradual elimination of Regulation Q, which limits the interest rates banks may pay on deposits).

One of the major objectives in the banking industry today is to increase core deposits. More and more banks are turning toward a segmented approach to marketing products—not only to increase core deposits from profitable new segments of the market such as newcomers, the elderly, and young professionals, but also to hold onto *existing* customer bases. Because studies have shown that the more services customers maintain with a bank, the less likely they are to switch financial institutions, banks are beginning to realize the significance of cross-selling to expand customers' relationships with the bank. Therefore, banks are focusing their attention on providing competitive services in strategic locations with a competent, well-trained staff.

First United's corporate goal, as stated in its Five-Year Action Plan, is by 1985 to have earned the image of being one of the best known and respected regional banking organizations in the Northeast. In addition, the bank's action plan outlines specific strategies to be taken with regard to *personnel* in order to achieve the corporate goal.

THE CUSTOMER SERVICE REPRESENTATIVE POSITION

A staff position has always existed in each of First United's branch offices whose primary job function is the opening and servicing of customer accounts. Originally designated as "new accounts," the nature of this position has changed considerably over the past five years, largely as a result of the following:

1. C.I.A.S.—the introduction of a *Customer Information Acquisition System,* a sophisticated computer system that provides instant access (through CRT terminals) to complete customer and account information files and requires extensive data input at the branch level.

2. More complex services—an increasingly complex array of services, from IRAs to money mar-

ket accounts, discount brokerage, and variable rate loans, whose features and benefits must be well understood and articulately explained to the customer upon first identifying the customer's need for the service.

3. Cross-selling—the increasing importance of cross-selling to obtain the customer's full banking relationship and, therefore, the development of the aggressive salesperson role associated with the position.

Aware of the changing nature of the new accounts position—a seemingly overnight transformation from a clerical/secretarial position into a sales-oriented position—senior management changed the job title in 1981 from new accounts to "customer service representative" (CSR), a title deemed by those who held the position as being more reflective of the actual job functions. Recognizing, however, that a change in the position title was nothing more than a surface, symbolic change, management developed a new profile for a First United customer service representative:

- Salesminded

- Customer-oriented

- Career-oriented

- Work-experienced

First United then included the following statement as part of its action plan: "To meet the challenges ahead for both the industry and our bank, it is crucial that we hire higher level, more work-experienced people. Moreover, we must give them extensive training and compensate them based on these principles and expectations for performance." As a result of the strategy proposed in the action plan, the following series of actions were taken in regard to the CSR position between 1981 and 1983.

1. Upgrading and division of the CSR position (1981). The job level of the CSR (job level being indicative of both the range of responsibility and salary potential) was upgraded from level 4 to level 7, with across-the-board salary increases being granted. In addition, the senior CSR position was created and designated as a level 10, with the primary difference in level resulting from the quasi-supervisory ability and lending authority a senior CSR would possess. Senior CSR personnel were to be located in smaller, rural offices where it was not feasible from a cost standpoint to have an assistant branch manager. These employees were to be "fast-trackers" who could fill in for the manager when he or she was out making commercial calls. Significant to note in both job descriptions is the consideration given to both sales and operational requirements of the job.

2. Training (1981–1983). The following training was provided to every CSR at First United over a two-year period:
   a. Selling skills and customer relations training. An intensive three-day program was developed to refresh basic customer relations skills and introduce professional selling techniques. Steps of the selling function were taught (the warmup, probing, recommendations, handling objections, closing the sale) using behavior modeling with experiential video role-play.

b. Advanced CSR training. A modular program was designed to refresh product knowledge and reinforce operational procedures. Fifty two-hour modules also acquainted the CSRs with other division/department functions and personnel within the bank.

3. Implementation of a cross-selling measurement system (1982). After the termination of both a manual sales tracking system and a sales incentive program in 1980, no system existed for measuring accurately the sales ability of the CSR. The introduction of an automated sales tracking system in 1982 permitted tracking of monthly and year-to-date sales performance at the individual, branch, regional area, and division levels. However, no monetary sales incentive program was reinstated.

4. CSR job requirements study (1982–1983). Developed by an outside research firm and administered by the personnel department, this survey asked the CSR to rank, in order of importance or frequency (1) work elements or tasks within the CSR job and (2) abilities required to perform the CSR job. The purpose of the study was two-fold: (1) to validate a pre-employment test thought by personnel to measure traits, abilities, and attitudes considered necessary for "success" as a CSR, and (2) to aid the periodic review of the CSR description for accuracy. At the conclusion of the study, the personnel department summarized its findings and presented the data to the appropriate officers of the bank. Results indicated that for *both* the junior (level 7) and senior level CSR (level 10), the five most frequently performed tasks were

as follows: answering telephone inquiries/taking messages; explaining available services; assisting customers with account problems; selling customers *other* bank services; and getting to know customers by name. However, in terms of the abilities required to perform the CSR job, the findings indicated a difference in perceptions between the two levels. For the level 7 CSR, the following represents the top five abilities required: ability to handle customer problems; ability to work with, and get along with, other people; ability to remain calm and pleasant at all times; ability to pay attention to detail; ability to learn new procedures quickly. For the senior level CSR, the top five required abilities were perceived to be as follows: ability to handle customers' problems; ability to pay attention to detail; ability to concentrate on work in spite of distractions; ability to remain calm and pleasant at all times; ability to handle problem customers.

5. The CST training needs analysis survey (1982–1983). Designed by skills training to identify specific skill and attitudinal factors in order to determine present and future training needs, this survey (using a questionnaire format) was given to every CSR *and* branch manager. Results of the survey indicated a high degree of recognition of the importance of training in *all* areas of the bank, given the "jack of all trades" nature of the CSR position. On a more specific note, many responses focused on the need for training in products, services, cross-selling, and time management.

FUTURE SALES TRAINING CONFERENCE

Upon reviewing the Training Needs Survey, Barry Vinson, senior vice-president for branch administration, called a conference of those officers directly responsible for training within the bank. Vinson recognized the importance of the CSR position in the future of First United and wanted to eliminate any real or potential obstacles that would dysfunctionally impact on the Five-Year Action Plan. Included in the discussion were Carol Morton, vice-president, training; Tom Hawkins, assistant vice-president, training; Courtney Wilson, training officer; and Bill Lowe, sales consultant for Sales Training Services, Inc., New York. The following discussion ensued.

Barry: Now that you've seen the latest sales tracking reports, I'm sure you'll agree that our CSRs need more sales training. Our cross-selling ratios have hovered around the 1.6 mark now for almost a year—we should be selling 3.5 services to every customer that walks through the door. I'm convinced our CSRs still don't know *how* to sell!

Courtney: Barry, *some* of our CSRs don't know how to sell. Most of them don't see their job as being a sales job. The surveys show us that. The CSR position is the catch-all position in the branch; every new product and every new procedure ends up in the CSRs' lap. They complain about not having time to cross-sell. They wait on customer after customer from 9:00 a.m. to 2:00 p.m., then spend the rest of the afternoon handling paperwork—inputting new account data on C.I.A.S., calling or writing overdrawn customers, ordering checks or branch supplies. Why, they even said that answering the phone is the most often performed task! Add to that the "little" assignments some of the branch managers give them, like doing credit workups, completing internal audit reports, and helping the tellers settle. Some of the managers can't seem to understand that the CSR isn't a personal secretary just because he or she can type. Throw in the fact that we pull them out of the branch on the average of once a week for some sort of training, and you've got one tough job!

Tom: I can't believe that's true, Courtney. Although I haven't been a CSR like you were, I've sat down with four of them over the past month to get some ideas for our new sales training program. Some of these kids *aren't* swamped — particularly in the smaller offices. The problem is that they aren't recognizing cross-selling opportunities. They give the customer just what he came in for, plus a handful of brochures and a promise to "be there" if the customer decides he wants something else. They just aren't selling! Maybe they just don't want to sell!

Carol: Tom, *why* don't they recognize cross-selling opportunities? I sat in on your sales course in 1981. Bill has even looked at it and says it covered all the important areas of sales training—three days of it, to boot. The CSRs' evaluations of the program were excellent. I even watched some of the video role-plays and some of those folks were taking to it like ducks to water!

Bill: Carol, the courseware was excellent. What went wrong wasn't with your program; it was that you didn't have a selling *system* in place. Look. . . it was the first time you had ever told the CSRs that they were your "professional sales force." When they were finished they were psyched to sell, but you sent them back to the branches, and the managers couldn't keep them psyched to sell. They didn't get any feedback or reinforcement from the managers. That's your problem in a nutshell.

Tom: But in all fairness to the managers,we didn't have a sales measurement system in place, so a manager had no objective way to tell how well his CSR was doing at that time. Now we do, so it should improve.

Bill: No, it won't improve until you train the managers how to be *sales managers.* Like I said, your problem wasn't the training program itself, it was a lack of a selling system. No actual goals were set for the CSRs. You didn't *tell* them you wanted at least a 3.0; you didn't even ask them what was reasonable! They got no feedback, good or bad, from the managers. You can't expect those CSRs to sell! Would *you,* if nobody followed up with you? What's their incentive?

Carol: How about the level and salary increase? That's a big incentive!

Courtney: I don't think the CSRs saw the salary increase as compensation for a new position. I think they thought the level increase was something long overdue. I don't mean to sound negative, but I still don't think that dispensing the training pill is going to cure this one. I think the problem is the job itself, not just the sales ability or inability of the people in it. Let's face it. We expect these people to be professional salespeople, but we haven't done anything to lighten up the operational load. We harp on them to sell, but deep down we still expect these folks to be computer data entry people, handholders, telephone operators, and personal secretaries. Look at some of those survey responses! I'm not saying that some of them don't need retraining in sales or that the managers don't need training in sales management; I'm sure they do. I'm saying that we've also got to take some of the dirty work out of that job.

Carol: You're saying we've got to come up with some ideas to streamline some of the operational duties of the CSR job to give them more *time* for selling?

Courtney: Yep. I think if we could look at some ways to redesign the job and *then* implement Bill's selling system then we might get a true picture of whether we even have the right people in the job. That's a whole different issue! I sure don't think our current performance appraisal can tell us! Of course, we'd have to work hand-in-hand with personnel.

Tom: That's one hell of a project, and I'm not so sure we can't go ahead with the sales training, anyway. After all, a lot of them are new to the bank and never got the sales training. What do you think, Barry? I really am concerned about this problem. The cross-selling ratio shouldn't be this low!

Barry: I'm meeting tomorrow with Andy Richardson from personnel to go over the results of the CSR Job Requirements Study. I think before we decide anything we should look more closely at the results from both surveys. By the way, the low cross-selling ratio isn't the problem; it's only the symptom! We have a great deal of work ahead of us.

1. You have determined that the CSRs' poor sales performance is directly related to the design of the CSR position itself and you realize that changing the CSR position may necessitate other structural changes in the branch. What recommendations for job redesign will you make to Mr. Vinson and Mr. Richardson?

2. Carol Morton mentioned that the CSRs' evaluations of the 1981 Sales Training Program were excellent. Therefore, she doesn't understand why the CSRs don't recognize opportunities for cross-selling. How valuable are the student evaluations for measuring the effectiveness of any training program?

3. Why is the correct diagnosis of any performance problem so vital?

27

COMPUTECH, INC.

In the continual race for superiority in the electronics industry, Computech, Inc. has managed to carve out a significant niche in the field of high-tech test and measurement instrumentation. Headquartered in California, the majority of the business of Computech resides in two technical areas: (1) computers and (2) research and design test instrumentation. In both areas, Computech professes to develop products that go beyond the norm in technical excellence. In fact, one of the foundation policies of Computech has been to avoid areas that do not allow room for significant advances in technology, regardless of the perceived financial value of the marketable device.

Over the years, this policy of aggressively remaining a step ahead of the competition has provided a relaxed forum for relations with Computech's customer base, due in most cases to the absence of direct, technologically equivalent competitors. The electronic instrumentation division of Computech still follows this ideology. The computer division, however, has been forced by market conditions to forego this policy in favor of endeavors in highly competitive markets. The divergent policies of the two groups have created some disruptive side-effects in the organization, from corporate headquarters down to the individual sales offices.

THE VIRGINIA SALES OFFICE

The Virginia sales office of Computech has followed the norm of offices cohabited by the instrumentation and the computer staff. Occasional problems have arisen due to the differing group policies and have been handled on an individual basis. Recently, however, in order to reduce the overloaded routine of the instrumentation district manager, the upper management determined that the Virginia district would be split, thus creating a new managerial position. At the same time, the computer district was consolidated into a larger district. Consequently, a managerial position was removed, and an experienced manager was left without a position. One of the more obvious solutions to the situation was to place the former computer manager in the new instrumentation manager's position. As such, he would have direct responsibility for four field engineers (engineering sales representatives) and one staff engineer (sales representative trainee).

Dick Jensen is the most experienced field engineer of the new group and is known for his laissez-faire approach to the job. Gary Metz is next in line in seniority but would probably rate lowest in perceived position power due to some behavioral instabilities. Eddie Wright, the perceived leader of the salesmen, follows in seniority, having been with Computech for 10 years. Next in line are Bob Adkins, with three years experience, and John Thomas, with nine months experience. Also, all of the staff except Bob and John have had prior working experience with various other companies in the electronics industry. Bob and John, on the other hand, have the benefit of being fresh from engineering programs with curriculums that taught methods that were not known, much less being used, during the other field engineers' schooling. All in all, the entire group possesses an advanced technological background in each of their respective disciplines of electrical engineering.

On the other hand, Ken Patterson, the new manager from the computer group, has been out of the mainstream of technical information for the past 10 years. Ken's career with Computech started as a sales representative. With rapid advancement, Ken achieved promotion after promotion until he reached the position of worldwide marketing manager. In this position, however, his driving personality turned against him, and he started his descent back down the corporate ladder. His present appointment is to a position just one level above his entry position over 25 years ago.

As might be expected, the transition did not occur without its share of problems. After three months in the position, Ken decided to call a meeting to clear the air of any misconceptions and to develop the proper power positioning for the entire staff. The following are representative excerpts from the staff meeting, which will attempt to portray the general atmosphere at hand.

Ken: I would like to accomplish several goals with this meeting. As I'm sure you know, there have been many statements floating around the office about me being here as your manager. It is true that I did not particularly desire to move from Atlanta to this area. It is not, however, true that I did not want to be part of this office.

Eddie: Oh, Ken, that rumor has spread, but we did not honestly believe that it was true; at least not all of it. . . . *(sly grin).*

Ken: Well, you can be sure of one thing. I needed a job and this is it. So, either way, we will make it work out *(joking mood—evident trace of determination).* Pressing on, I have noticed several areas where the past manager was lax in his duties.

Dick: That's a rather strong comment about Joe. Remember, he has been our peer, friend, and, more recently, boss for several years now.

Ken: Oh, I didn't mean anything against Joe personally, but he did leave several areas unorganized.

Eddie: Oh great! Is this when you pull out the shackles?

Ken: No, just the handbook. Listen, I'll admit that I'm not technically able to keep up with you guys, but I do have other things to offer—like experience. Right now you've been approaching the business from your individual ideas of what is correct. I'm going to show the "proper" way to sell. Oh, you may challenge me. I welcome that, but I will win. Remember, I'm holding all the bullets!

Bob: That's great, Ken, but where are we supposed to go with technical requirements? You admit that you won't be able to give much help there, and the next level doesn't always have the time. Also, what do you mean by the proper way to sell? Does that mean that what I've been doing up until now is wrong?

Ken: Hold on, Bob. My only goal is to make you the best salesman that you can be. That goes for all of you. With my coaching, you all possess the requirements to attain the highest level in your field and the spoils that accompany that position.

Gary: What about me? I was the top salesman last year. I hope that you don't plan to coach me, too!

Ken: Yes, Gary, you will all attend my weekly seminars. After all, we are all in this together.

John: I don't know if I should speak, but I really think that we are fortunate. I'm looking forward to working in these seminars.

Ken: Now that's the right attitude! Well then, let's get down to business.

The meeting continued with an outline of various programs and proposals for operating the office. Afterwards, Gary was noted as remarking, "If he wants to coach me, he's going to have to catch up with me first. I'm going to stay on the road constantly now." Dick gave the impression that he would attend the seminars to look good, but he still believed, in his case, the adage that "you can't teach an old dog new tricks." Eddie just does not believe that any of the new actions will ever take place. Bob simply doesn't know what to think except for wondering how to reduce his present level of stress associated with uncertainty. John, on the other hand, is excited about his new, close supervision. Finally, Ken appears to be oblivious to the apathy that surrounds him by his more experienced salesmen. Instead, he prefers to note John's enthusiasm as indicative of the group. In fact, Ken remarked as he passed the secretary, "I'm glad that's over. Maybe now we can start acting like a real sales office."

Obviously, however, Ken's problems have just begun. The major problem, lack of proper communication, is fostered by another problem—the conflicting styles of old (people-oriented) and new (job-oriented) management. Both the manager and his staff are making assumptions as to how the office should be run. The staff will defend its position from past record, while the new manager has stated his defense as his position of power. Sadly, the absolute validity of either defense is questionable but will still be held onto by the parties involved.

QUESTIONS

1. Do you feel that Ken Patterson has assumed the proper leadership role under the circumstances?

2. The communication path between the new manager and present staff seems to be hampered by obstructions from both directions. What are some of these obstructions and how may they be overcome?

28

NORTH AMERICAN MEDICAL SYSTEMS, INC.

North American Medical Systems, Inc. (NMS) was founded in the early 1960s by two data processing consultants, Travis Jackson and Charles Edwards. The company's initial operations were that of providing data processing services to hospitals and medical practices in northern Virginia and Maryland. As a pioneer in the use of computer technology in the health care business, the company grew rapidly until 1970 when it was bought by a large corporation that owned a chain of acute care hospitals. At this point, Mr. Jackson decided to leave the company to pursue other business interests, whereas Mr. Edwards continued to operate NMS as an independent subsidiary.

From 1970 through 1978, the company's basic business shifted away from hospital data processing operations toward the providing of management services to small- and medium-sized physician groups. As this transition occurred, total revenues reached $10 million, but company profitability declined dramatically. At this time, NMS had management contracts with 50 practices in 17 states from Virginia to California. The company had 200 employees, 150 of whom were located in the various offices the firm managed, with the remaining 50 providing administrative and support functions from the headquarters in northern Virginia.

At the insistence of the parent company, a new comptroller was hired in July 1978. The new comptroller, John Green, was 35 years old and was a Certified Public Accountant with 10-years experience in financial management positions. He was given the responsibility for updating the existing accounting system and providing improved financial information.

The company continued to experience significant losses, however, and little long-range planning was being done.

Despite a continued growth in revenues, in June 1980 the company's founder and president, Charles Edwards, was fired by the parent company. The major reason given was the apparent lack of strategies and plans designed to cure the company's financial problems, and the feeling that a new approach had to be found to turn the company around.

From June through December 1980, the parent company searched for a new president while NMS was being managed by John Green and the company's operations vice-president, Fred Hanks. During this interim period, NMS stabilized its expansion efforts and began to evaluate more carefully the potential profitability of new management contracts. John Green assumed responsibility for the review of all new management contracts as to policy, cost projections, and legal considerations. Existing contracts were also evaluated, and it was noted that some were not producing an adequate gross margin to cover allocated support and administrative costs. In addition, it became clear to Green that the physician group management business, if run on the same basis as in the past, could *not* be made profitable. This was due to the high travel, communications, and centralized support costs that were associated with the national dispersion of small, independent offices.

In January of 1981, a new president, Robert Peters, was hired. Mr. Peters' previous position had been regional marketing vice-president for a major pharmaceutical firm. He was 51 years old and had spent his entire business career in sales and marketing positions. It was expected that his lack of experience in the areas of finance and health care management would not be a detriment to the process of continuing the company's past growth.

A NEW STRATEGY—
IMPLEMENTATION AND PROBLEMS

Shortly after joining NMS, Bob Peters called a meeting of all company managers, including John Green, to establish a formal corporate business plan. At the start of the meeting, Mr. Peters made it clear that he saw NMS's future as a continuation of its current business. Immediately John Green questioned this approach. "Rather than base our corporate plan on the company's current business, shouldn't we begin identifying the company's strengths and weaknesses, and try to fit the strengths into those business activities where we see an opportunity for profit?"

Bob Peters responded by asking, "How many business plans have you prepared?" When John answered that he had not prepared a comprehensive business plan, Mr. Peters concluded, "Until you've had that experience, we will prepare the plan my way."

Over the following one-and-a-half years, Bob Peters and John Green continued to disagree on many issues. Peters blamed the company's continuing losses on errors in the financial statements and overly restrictive accounting policies. He overruled John's rejection of several new management contracts that, in John Green's opinion, would not have provided adequate profitability. He rejected any suggestions that existing contracts should be renegotiated to improve profits, pushing instead for significant cost reductions in all areas.

Bob Peters' management style became more and more autocratic. He insisted on signing every disbursement check himself, and he hired several managers whose primary strength seemed to revolve around agreeing with Bob Peters. He brought in an outside financial consultant to assist John Green in bringing the accounting system "out of the dark ages." He raised management by intimidation to new heights by requiring that all employees sign a new, more restrictive employment contract.

John Green continued to press for structural changes in the company's business that would enhance profitability, but his memorandums setting out his suggestions were categorized as reactionary and impractical by Peters. When contact with the parent company was proposed by John in an effort to settle some theoretical accounting questions, Peters forbade any further communication of that type without his express approval.

John realized that his future with NMS was in serious jeopardy. Every attempt by John to reconcile philosophical differences with Peters had been exhausted. It appeared to be a case of Peters being convinced that his own strategy was appropriate and not to be challenged by a young upstart like John Green.

Finally, on April 27, 1982, John Green was called into Bob Peters' office. Mr. Peters began the conversation. "You know, John, we've had many discussions and disagreements over the past year and a half. Obviously, this type of friction is not in the best interests of the company. It is clear that one of us will have to go. Therefore, I expect your letter of resignation to be on my desk first thing tomorrow morning."

QUESTIONS

1. Given the obvious conflict between John Green and Bob Peters, suggest some strategies that might have been utilized to minimize the ef-

fect(s) of the conflict. Discuss the advantages
and disadvantages of each strategy.

2. What are the primary reasons why the conflict
ended as it did?

29

WESTERN UTILITY AND POWER SUPPLY

The Western Utility and Power Supply is a large corporation providing power for approximately six million people. A major expenditure for this company is the purchase of fuel for its power stations. This necessitates negotiations with vendors outside the company as well as various other departments within the company. The fuel purchasing and quality control group has 10 members reporting to a director. One individual supervises coal purchases, another supervises oil purchases, one deals with transportation of fuel, and another deals with the storage of the fuel. The other members of this group are involved in economic studies and special projects that develop from time to time. This subgroup reports to one supervisor, Walter Jackson, a young and well-respected man in the organization.

Although only recently promoted to the supervisory position, it did not take Jackson long to realize that his staff consisted of many varied and distinct personalities. Lucy Simmons, for example, is a dedicated career woman who has been with Western for six years and seems to thrive in the organization setting. Then there is Bob Henry, a determined and sometimes frustrating individual with two years service, who feels very uncomfortable in the structured, rule-oriented policy and procedure world of Western. In addition, there is Gloria Williams, who feels that she is overworked and underpaid. Although she has only been with Western four years, Gloria feels that, without her, the entire organization would fall apart. She tells everyone how hard she has to work, especially correcting all of Bob Henry's mistakes (whom she considers totally incompetent).

Both Lucy and Gloria seem to enjoy the organization background and are careful to follow each rule and policy to the end. Lucy was in the process of completing requirements for a Master of Science in Engineering degree and is the top person on Jackson's staff. While Lucy is diligent and hard-working, Gloria just likes being in on everything. Her day is spent making sure she gets the low-down on everyone throughout the department. She has a better information system than the FBI and a communications network that would put AT&T to shame! Gloria recently received an Associate Degree in Psychology, which, according to her, qualified her for many responsible jobs, better than the one she has at Western.

Bob Henry is just the opposite of Lucy Simmons. He tends to pay less attention to policies and procedures, dislikes going to meetings, and feels too much time is spent on "fluff and puff." All the rigid structure frustrates and annoys him. He was not used to going through all the various levels of supervision to get the job done, since he was in charge of a medium-size store before he came to Western. Although Simmons and Henry are complete opposites, each respects the other's abilities and no problems occur between the two.

PRELUDE TO CONFRONTATION

Bob and Gloria did not like each other from the outset, with the first minor skirmish occurring less than a month after Bob's arrival on the scene. He had started a project, only to find Gloria intervening while he was at lunch. When he asked her sternly what she was doing, she replied that she was about to complete the project. Bob, very frustrated, said nothing and just walked away. Later that day, he was called into the director's office and was told that he should stop fighting with Gloria and be a team player. Bob said that he did not know he was fighting with Gloria.

For a short period of time, Gloria forgot about Bob, primarily because she had been having trouble with some of the girls in another section of the department. In fact, for a while, Bob and Gloria were actually friendly, but the peace did not last. Occasionally, the director would say things to Bob that Bob knew could only have come from Gloria. He was being blamed for everything that did not work well, from messing up the files to supplying incorrect information on fuel purchases.

Gloria also kept the time files, keeping an especially close eye on Bob's activities, although he did not abuse the system and informed his supervisor, Mr. Jackson, when he had to be out of the office. Bob, usually a happy fellow, had now become very defensive and somewhat arrogant. His anger and frustrations were beginning to have a shotgun effect. His displaced anger flashed and was often directed at the director and manager of the department. He began to dislike his job and hated to come in to the office after a weekend. He would wonder what Gloria was going to do to him *that* day.

Once in a while he would mention his problems to Jackson, who would attempt to relieve Bob's frustrations. Jackson tried, but could not convince Bob that Gloria's attacks were having no effect on the people who counted. Nevertheless, Bob's tolerance of Gloria seemed to be fading fast.

CONFLICT IN PROGRESS

Not long after his discussion with Jackson, Bob Henry learned that Gloria Williams had been telling everyone in the office that he was worthless and that she had to do all the work and pick up the slack. This infuriated

Bob, because if the truth were known, he had to step in on several occasions to complete many of Gloria's tasks. For example, he discovered that errors on the fuel purchases were being attributed to him by Gloria. He was convinced that Gloria's allegations had cost him a promotion. The thought of working with her for the next 40 years of his working life was too much for him to bear. He had never experienced this type of problem before, and he just could not figure out what to do.

Finally, the volcano erupted when Bob caught wind of the fact that Gloria had gone to the manager, George Anders, to complain about Bob's poor attitude and work performance. It seems that many of the fuel orders contained errors that went undiscovered until it was too late to correct them. Since Gloria was assisting the manager in finding the guilty party, her choice was Bob. The only problem was that Bob had not had any connection with the fuel orders that month. Jackson had pulled Bob off of that particular job because of the growing tensions between Gloria and Bob.

When the manager sought out both Jackson and Bob on the errors, it was probably fortunate that he caught up with Jackson first. Bob had a habit of acting (or reacting) first and thinking about it later. Jackson explained the situation to Anders. He pointed out the growing animosity between Bob and Gloria and said that Bob had no part in the fuel orders for that period. George, satisfied with Jackson's explanation, terminated his search for Bob. Jackson, successful at diffusing this bomb, found another waiting in his office as a seething Bob Henry opened fire. Poor Jackson was wondering if his promotion to supervisor was worth it. Earlier in the week, Bob had opened up after Gloria had misinterpreted Bob's actions. Some errors had slipped through and were caught by the vice-president. When Gloria became very upset, Bob told her that it was no big deal and corrections could easily be made. Gloria snapped at Bob, who was quite surprised at her response to his sympathetic gesture. Jackson asked Bob what went on, and Bob told him about the incident. Although he had his faults, Bob was truthful and even admitted that he may have gone too far in announcing that the vice-president was not a god, and when he became perfect, he (Bob) would start to worry! The conversation that followed between Jackson and Henry was lively, to say the least.

Henry: I've had it with Gloria Williams and that jerk we call a manager *(Anders)*! I have had to work with her for two years, waiting for the axe to fall. I have tried every way I can think of to get along with her. What else is there for me to do? I hate coming to work for fear of what she may have cooked up for today. I don't need her or this stupid job. I have done all right for 24 years without both and will continue to do so. I am tired of dodging bullets and back-stabbing. She is the one who cannot do the job, not me. She is too busy telling everyone how good she is, and how all the vice-presidents are depending on her vital paperwork. I want out!

Jackson: Calm down, Bob! I have talked with George Anders and he knows the whole story. You have nothing to fear and I promise the situation will be straightened out.

Henry: Sure, until the next time Gloria decides to hassle me. I am always being accused of feuding with her. The only problem is that I never know when the feuds are occurring. If I am feuding with her, she should have the common decency to inform me—not to leave me in the dark. It might be fun, and at least I could defend myself!

Jackson: Don't get so excited, Bob! George and I will talk to Gloria and resolve the whole situation once and for all.

Henry: Walt, I'm just not convinced. As far as I'm concerned, Anders will give Gloria a tap on the wrist so he won't offend her too much. Then Gloria will complain that I am feuding with her again and the whole cycle starts over. Six weeks from now we'll be having the same discussion. I'm tired of the aggravation, and the money isn't worth it. You don't have to listen to her because you're the boss. She is almost on the same level with me now and, at the rate she is moving, I will soon be reporting to her! There's no way I can handle that!

Jackson: I cannot change her personality or behavior; that is just the way she is! If you were in my position, how would you handle the situation?

Henry: If I could, I would transfer her to another country! Seriously though, all I want is to keep her off my back. I'm tired of looking over my shoulder for her. If it means leaving the company, it's worth it for my peace of mind.

Again, Jackson assured Bob that he was going to talk to Gloria and asked Bob if he wanted to have a face-to-face meeting with her. Bob indicated this would be a bad idea because it might just turn into a shouting match. From his standpoint, with Gloria's mouth, he would not stand a chance. Bob was smiling again, and the veins were no longer popping out of his neck. Jackson was three-for-three in handling explosive situations and felt he could qualify for a job with the bomb squad—it might be safer, because he still had to talk to Gloria.

Both George Anders and Walter Jackson spoke to

Gloria, who was visibly shaken by the lecture. For weeks, Bob and Gloria eyed each other, but no real problems occurred between the two. Bob felt better for the time being; he felt he had some upper-level support that he was not sure of before. He now felt he could deal with Gloria if she started any more problems because he would not be standing alone. He was bolstered by the knowledge that several of his coworkers were aware of Gloria's behavior from past episodes, and they were very sympathetic toward him, even volunteering to speak out on his behalf.

THE END OR JUST THE BEGINNING?

In the coming weeks, Gloria again attempted to stir up trouble, but Bob was able to handle the situation without any assistance from Jackson or Anders. Nevertheless, Bob Henry was still uneasy about this relationship and wondered if the relative calm would last or if another major confrontation was on the way. Jackson, of course, was carefully monitoring the situation since he didn't want to lose either employee.

QUESTIONS

1. Several methods were employed to manage the conflict between Bob Henry and Gloria Williams. What were these methods and was the final attempt to resolve the conflict likely to be successful?

2. Discuss the effects of the conflict on Henry and whether he is likely to return to his former self. What are the consequences for the firm as a whole?

30

BIG VALLEY
NATIONAL BANK

Big Valley Bankshares, Inc. is a statewide bank holding company. Its headquarters and largest affiliate bank are located in the agricultural and mineral-rich region of North Carolina. Big Valley has developed a reputation as a sound, conservative financial institution, firmly embedded in the predominantly rural areas of the state. During the 1970s, more lenient regulations regarding statewide holding companies precipitated Big Valley's expansion into new markets. The company began to acquire smaller banks in major metropolitan centers throughout North Carolina. It has since grown to be one of the largest bank holding companies in the state.

COMPANY BACKGROUND

Big Valley National Bank (BVNB) of Winston was acquired by the holding company in 1972. The local bank was formed in 1964 as the First City National Bank and prospered under the direction of a young and aggressive management team. With most of the large North Carolina banks headquartered in Winston, the market was thought to be saturated with banks. However, through several innovative pricing schemes designed to undercut the area banks' fees, First City began attracting loyal customers from the competition. Big Valley was naturally impressed with First City's growth and the potential for new commercial business in the Winston market. Therefore, Big Valley decided to purchase the $50 million bank.

Today, Big Valley National Bank of Winston has assets of $150 million. However, most of the original top management has moved on to pursue other goals. Most recently, the senior credit officer and senior operations officer have transferred to the holding company. Of those who remain in senior management, or those recently elevated to this level, many were once clerks with First City. Indeed, one of the advantages to be reaped from working for a small firm is the opportunity to advance rapidly, given the proper initiative and fortunate timing.

Among BVNB's four present divisions is the financial division. In the past, the senior operations officer managed all of the functions that now comprise the financial division: accounting, purchasing and bank services, and financial services. Additionally, this individual oversaw all of the areas contained in the operations center, including proof and transit, bookkeeping, and item processing. However, today the latter departments have been absorbed by the operations of BVNB's regional affiliates, forming a holding company-managed unit. The financial division is now headed by the vice-president and controller. All the departments reporting to the controller are managed by recently promoted (within the last year) officers.

FINANCIAL SERVICES

Financial services became a formal entity five years ago and consisted of one "glorified" secretary who was responsible for taking customer investment orders, setting "Jumbo CD" rates, bookkeeping, typing entries, and calculating cash management account balances.

Two years later the department staff doubled, with one clerk and one exempt employee (nonofficer).

With the departure of the senior operations officer one year ago, the controller decided that several areas that performed different functions but shared a commercial emphasis and contact with the bank's best customers, should be lumped together under financial services. The areas were wire transfer, safekeeping and paying agent, and the old financial services.

The changes that were occurring at this time were beneficial to some employees and detrimental to others. One employee who was lost in the shuffle was Mary Jo Parker. Mary Jo began working for First City 13 years ago as a teller. She had originally lived in Tryon, North Carolina, where she had previous teller experience, before moving to Winston. In 1977, Barton Pierce, the senior operations officer, selected Mary Jo to perform a job that required certain specialization, reporting directly to him. Mary Jo would learn to safekeep customers' securities and maintain paying agent accounts. She was chosen for the job because she had done excellent work in the branch and had indicated a desire to advance.

In 1979, during Mary Jo's annual review, Barton told her that he expected her area to grow, and when it did, it would grow beneath her. In addition, Barton bestowed upon her the lofty title of "safekeeping and municipal services coordinator." All of this attention was encouraging to Mary Jo, but during the next two years she gradually became frustrated because she was continually being passed over for promotion to officer level. She was aware of her shortcomings, yet there were other women who joined First City at the same time as she who were already officers. Furthermore, Barton had given her excellent ratings in her performance reviews, thus making the whole situation more confusing.

Barton was well aware of Mary Jo's hopes, but he also knew that she lacked several qualities required of an officer. First, Mary Jo had never really learned to write beyond a fifth-grade level. In addition, she had difficulty pronouncing common words such as "municipal bond." These deficiencies hindered Mary Jo since most of her work entailed corresponding with the bank's best customers. Unfortunately, Barton never told Mary Jo of his misgivings; instead, he continued to give her commendable ratings and comments.

In 1981, just before Barton left BVNB for the holding company, Mary Jo was told to report to Tom Blackstone, the controller. Mary Jo was a little perturbed by this event, since she was used to reporting directly to Barton, and Tom was not as high ranking an officer as Barton. At this same time, Tom Blackstone was filling the vacancy of financial assistant, who would be in charge of the two-person financial services department. He had chosen Larry Carson, a young trainee who had progressed rapidly in the branch system and was enthusiastic about going downtown, "where the action is."

During Larry's first year in financial services, he continued to progress and seek new responsibilities. When Barton left BVNB, Tom decided that Larry would manage the new, enlarged financial services division. Larry was promoted to officer rank, and Mary Jo was told to report to Larry.

Mary Jo, who had been miffed when asked to report to Tom, was livid at this most recent development. To work for Larry, she felt, was a slap in her face. Furthermore, it clarified management's attitude toward her all of these years. Mary Jo would also have to move from her office, in which she had worked alone since 1977, to a new office, to be shared with the wire transfer clerk. She had helped fill in as wire transfer clerk years ago, and it appeared to her that she was regressing to her old duties. In addition, she would be working with two clerks who, between them, had less years with BVNB than Mary Jo. Finally, Mary Jo's title would change to "financial services clerk" to make it conform to the job titles of the other employees in similar positions. In an effort to appease Mary Jo, Tom placed her in a higher salary range.

After meeting with Tom and Larry and discussing the changes taking place, Mary Jo's mood changed considerably. She began complaining constantly, although she had been known to complain periodically in the past. Her displeasure was so evident that people outside the department and division could recognize it. Others frequently overheard Mary Jo maintaining that she had been demoted.

Within the department, Mary Jo would not blatantly attempt to irritate or confront Larry. Instead, she would burden him with simple problems that she had handled alone in the past. Any time that she would call a customer on the telephone she would ask Larry if he would prefer to talk with them, "since you are an officer."

Tom, who was at this time promoted to division head, was cognizant of Mary Jo's feelings toward her new status. He was also aware that he was far too busy to oversee her himself. Tom expressed this and some other ideas to Larry. One thought was that Mary Jo would have to be told that she would most likely never become an officer at BVNB. Another point was that Mary Jo must learn to be neater and reduce her number of typing errors. Finally, Mary Jo would relinquish some of her recent duties and pick up others. Regardless of the anxiety associated with these suggestions, the bottom line was that Mary Jo would have to become more productive.

Larry felt caught in the middle. On one hand, he realized the importance of the overall departmental and organizational goals, and he was excited to be given this opportunity. On the other hand, Larry knew that Mary Jo had been led down an enchanted path. She had always been allowed to believe she would advance and be recognized, only to have her illusions shattered abruptly. Larry was committed to making the department effective and efficient; this meant that the personnel would have to work harmoniously. Could Mary Jo, who had really been clipping coupons for years, adapt to new duties? She must be cross-trained in the functions of the other jobs in order to fill in when others were absent. Overall, Larry realized the need for specialized skills if his department was to contribute to the overall performance of BVNB. His handling of Mary Jo's situation would certainly be a test of his effectiveness as a manager.

QUESTIONS

1. Is there any way that Larry can improve Mary Jo's performance in the financial services division?

2. What problems will arise due to Tom Blackstone's requirements and Larry Carson's expectations for the department? How should Larry deal with these problems?

31

SOUTHERN COMMERCIAL BANK AND TRUST

Southern Commercial Bank and Trust is a statewide bank holding company headquartered in Atlanta. Southern offers its customers a full range of deposit and loan services from over 100 offices around Georgia. Currently, the bank is one of the state's largest financial institutions with assets in excess of $3 billion and deposits of $2.5 billion. Twenty years ago, however, Southern was the state's largest bank and was known as the "blue-blood" bank. If you had money, you banked with Southern. The bank also had a strong corporate lending department, which further enhanced its image.

It was in the early 1970s that Southern Commercial began to falter. An acquisition in southern Georgia proved to be a terrible mistake as a large portion of its commercial loan portfolio defaulted. Back in Atlanta, Southern's new 20-story headquarters was partially completed when the contractor declared bankruptcy. The new contractor's expenses were considerably higher than the original estimate and resulted in a strained financial position for the bank. To make matters worse, the 1974–75 recession caused many of the bank's loans to be written off. Deposits and assets declined dramatically, as did the bank's reputation. The final blow came when Southern's name appeared on the comptroller of the currency's troubled bank list.

Miraculously, through tight management policy, Southern survived. While the bank failed to experience the growth of its major competitors, it did manage to rebuild its deposit and loan base and eventually began to expand. Today, although no longer Georgia's premier bank, Southern Commercial Bank and Trust is enjoying record earnings and a strong financial position.

Recently Southern merged with another Georgia bank to become the state's largest financial institution, with assets of $6.95 billion, 20 percent larger than its closest competitor. Significant advantages would result from such a merger—a higher legal lending limit, an extensive branch network, and major cost reductions. However, the employees fear that one of the first savings to be implemented will be staff reductions. While management stated from the beginning that there would be no terminations, most of the personnel are skeptical. Comparisons with other banks of approximately the same size as the "new" Southern Commercial Bank and Trust revealed that those institutions operated with approximately 2000 fewer employees. Needless to say, many Southern employees are experiencing feelings of tension and anxiety.

CORPORATE PLANNING

The corporate planning department is one of four departments comprising Southern's corporate planning and control division and has been actively involved in the merger from the beginning. The other departments are corporate tax, corporate accounting, and profitability analysis. Corporate planning has the responsibility for five functions—strategic planning, budget, financial analysis, mergers and acquisitions, and market research. Floyd Anderson, a senior vice-president, heads up the area.

Market research is a relative newcomer to the corporate planning department, having only been a part of the department for three and a half years. It was formerly under the auspices of the marketing division. The transfer was the result of a management decision to "reward" Floyd Anderson for his exceptional performance as leader of an internal profitability study by increasing his responsibilities. The research group (a director and three analysts) moved to corporate planning's third-floor quarters shortly thereafter. When first notified of the transfer, the research staff was somewhat apprehensive of the change. However, Anderson assured them that it was a great opportunity since their responsibilities would be increasing from a retail function (pricing, promotion, and performance of consumer services) to a corporate function. This potential for growth mollified the staff. However, one year later, little change in duties had occurred.

In addition, Anderson transferred the research director and one analyst to another department within the division. He promised the two remaining analysts—Betsy Robertson and Sarah Thompson—that in the near future he would fill the other positions with experts from the research field. Here again, Anderson assured Betsy and Sarah not to worry, that great opportunities abounded—trips to the bank's regions across the state, involvement in corporate-wide projects, and classes and seminars on product development. Although they hoped the situation would improve, Betsy and Sarah were becoming more and more doubtful that Anderson would follow through on his promises.

Their first year in the corporate planning department had been a frustrating one. Although market research was located on the same floor as the rest of the department, it was physically separated from the others. Because of research's unique function, there was very little contact with other members of the division. As a result, the staff never felt as if it were really a part of corporate planning.

Betsy Robertson had been a Southern employee for 12 years, all of which she had spent in market research. Before joining the bank, she had been a research assistant at the Federal Reserve Bank in Atlanta. Betsy was now the senior analyst, and it was her goal to one day be the director of Southern's research group. Betsy had a good reputation at the bank—she was well-respected for her knowledge and skills and known for her good-natured personality.

Sarah was the newest research analyst in the department, joining the bank only three months before the transfer to corporate planning. While this was Sarah's first job after college, she quickly learned her responsibilities and proved to be a conscientious employee. As Sarah and Betsy were the only women in market research, they became good friends and developed an excellent working relationship.

After the personnel changes, Betsy informed Anderson that she would like to be considered for the vacant director's position. He replied that Betsy would *not* be viewed as a possible candidate because she lacked the necessary experience. Believing in her qualifications and experience, Betsy proceeded to the personnel department to apply for the opening anyway. Nevertheless, Anderson remained adamant in his position that she was unqualified and refused to interview her. However, since there was still no director, and Betsy was the senior research analyst, she was responsible for reporting to Anderson on research issues.

Anderson made it difficult for Betsy·to carry out these responsibilities by being detached and aloof. "I'm too busy" or "See me later" were frequent responses to her requests for his time. As a result, morale within the research group was low, and while Betsy and Sarah tried to maintain their work standards, performance was hurt by Anderson's lack of attention. Betsy and Sarah's only hope was that when Anderson did hire someone as research director, the individual would truly be an expert in the field—one who would bring challenging and innovative ideas on board as well as stand up to Anderson.

It took 11 months, but Anderson finally followed through on his promise to hire a research director. Charlotte Lawrence came to Southern from one of its major competitors. Anderson was very pleased with his selection; although Charlotte had no research experience, she had come from Georgia's top bank and that was all that mattered. Unfortunately, there was confusion from day one. The memo announcing Charlotte's hiring stated that she would be head of product/market research while Betsy would continue as manager of market research. Betsy was especially surprised as she had not been directly assigned any market research responsibilities by Anderson.

Betsy and Sarah soon began to resent Charlotte. She didn't socialize, was cold, and did not encourage participation. Charlotte delegated all tasks to Betsy and Sarah, then claimed the results as her own. This was all very different from the research group Betsy and Sarah were used to—one where credit was given where due. However, they realized there was little they could do about the situation other than continue to do their jobs and document all their work. Charlotte wanted the tasks accomplished, and aside from that, she wanted little to do with Betsy and Sarah.

Anderson also had little time for the research staff. After Charlotte was hired he established a formal communication chain: Anderson to Lawrence to Robertson to Thompson. He only wanted contact with those who reported directly to him. The chain was to be followed strictly. If Anderson had a project for Sarah, he told Charlotte, who told Betsy, who then relayed the message to Sarah.

About one year after Charlotte's arrival, Southern

began confidential merger discussions. As Anderson was responsible for mergers and acquisitions, he was actively involved from the beginning, collecting and analyzing data pertaining to the merger. After five months of hard work, the banks reached agreement on merger terms, and a public statement announcing their intention was made. After both boards of directors blessed the combination, an organizational study was undertaken to select the key players—division and department heads and eventually their subordinates— and to determine their responsibilities. Anxiety and tension were obvious as employees, especially those in high positions, worried about what would happen.

At Southern, resumes and biographical sketches were to be developed on all employees. The level to which this information was gathered varied among divisions. In the corporate planning and control division, biographical sketches and summaries of responsibilities were requested for those persons on the two levels below the controller, the head of the division. For Anderson, this included himself; Charlotte; Tom Smithson, who was manager of mergers and acquisitions; and Bob Gordon, who was in charge of the financial analysis/budget area. Anderson quickly assembled the desired information and turned it in to his boss. He felt very confident that he would fare well in the new organization since he perceived himself to be one of Southern's brightest officers. The only question in his mind was what new responsibilities he would receive once the merger was consummated.

The other department heads in the division were not quite as hasty as Anderson in turning in their information. They felt that it was their responsibility as managers to protect the interests of all of their employees, not just a selected few. Betsy and Sarah, aware that they had been excluded from Floyd's report, caught wind of this. When Betsy confronted Anderson about this his reply was, "I was only requested to collect the information on those who report directly to me." While Betsy knew that this was true, she was disappointed in the person who was allegedly her leader. No more was mentioned, although several weeks later Anderson requested (through Charlotte) Betsy's biographical sketch.

Betsy and Sarah were becoming more and more frustrated. Both had worked hard on the merger, supplying much information on Southern's market areas, customers, and products, and now they were being ignored. So far, they had received no word on the status of the market research group. Through the grapevine they heard about what was happening with respect to other departments, although nothing was ever said about corporate planning or Floyd Anderson. Betsy and Sarah felt that Anderson wanted to keep the research function under his realm although he never mentioned that or anything about the organizational study to them.

Finally, from a source within the division, Betsy and Sarah learned that corporate planning and control would be called the "finance division" in the new organization. Word was also out that the major department heads had been assigned responsibilities and that Anderson's had been sharply curtailed. Still no word from Anderson to his research associates. Betsy and Sarah are hesitant to initiate a discussion with him. Long ago he lost his credibility with these two, and they found it difficult to believe what he says.

In early June the first organizational chart for the new bank was distributed to all employees. Two days after the chart was published, Charlotte asked Betsy if she had seen it. Betsy replied, "Yes, but what does this mean for us?" Charlotte answered, "I don't know. Floyd and I want to keep you in planning." Betsy then asked, "Why hasn't Floyd taken the time to talk with Sarah and me and explain what's going on? If we understood what's behind his actions, maybe we wouldn't be so quick to criticize." Angrily Charlotte responded, "It's a two-way street; you could have asked!"

QUESTIONS

1. Betsy and Sarah are frustrated by their lack of interaction with Floyd Anderson. However, they find that when they do communicate, one of the parties is immediately put on the defensive. What has led to this breakdown, and how can the situation be improved?

2. How can the autocratic Floyd Anderson improve his credibility with his subordinates in the research group?

32

THE T. H. MACKELL COMPANY

The T. H. Mackell Company, located on the outskirts of Chicago in the suburban town of Wheaton, Illinois, is the perfect example of a Horatio Alger rags to riches story. Founded by a native of the suburb in 1866, it began as a one-room storefront with three employees. Under the direction of four generations of the Mackell family it grew into a diversified multinational corporation operating in more than 50 countries with over 5,000 employees. Primarily engaged in the manufacture and sale of ethical pharmaceuticals and consumer products, the company occupied a position of respect and admiration both in the community and throughout the world.

SCIENTIFIC AND TECHNICAL INFORMATION DEPARTMENT

Subsequent to a recent company-wide reorganization plan, T. H. Mackell was divided into seven major divisions. Among these various divisions, research and development was the fastest growing one, as evidenced by both physical and budget size. In the past year alone, research and development (R&D) expenditures had reached $30 million, and combined R&D totals for the past 10 years totaled more than $170 million. Due to the ever-increasing size of the division, several departments had undergone substantial reorganization in recent years in an attempt to allocate resources to areas where the greatest need had developed. One particular department, scientific and technical information (STID), had earned the reputation as the "department on wheels," due to the constant shuffling of its resources—both human and physical office space.

The director of the department, Dr. Kenneth Barton, was widely known in the company for his expertise in handling the scientific aspects of the litigation resulting from the marketing of an arthritis drug. Although the drug had been off the market for several years, suits continued to pour in, alleging permanent disability as a result of its use. Despite his success in dealing with the continuing litigation, Dr. Barton was generally given low marks as a manager, due to his crony method of management. For females to advance, it was necessary to become one of "Ken's girls," a phrase he often used in conversations with them and to those outside the department. As a result, the two female managers in the area were afforded little respect elsewhere in the company. Males were either his pals or his enemies. Hired as director of the department some 18 years ago, Dr. Barton still retained the exact same title and position. This was the only open acknowledgement of his shortcomings as a leader.

The scientific and technical information department was comprised of five separate sections that reported to Barton. He in turn reported to Dr. Steven Heath, vice-president, office of administrative services. This arrangement had been modified, discarded, revitalized, and reinstated numerous times. In the past one and a half years, the information analysis section of the department had undergone two separate moves in physical quarters. Rumors through the grapevine dubbed the section the stepchild of the department because information services, another section of the department, had been increasing its scope and duties.

The information analysis section, headed by Mr. Dan Dorsey as manager, consisted of seven employees: Mr. Tom Perkins, Mr. J. W. Tabor, Mr. Tyrone Jensen,

Mrs. Alice Whitt, Ms. Sally Caldwell, and Mrs. April Groves. Mr. Dorsey, 54, was a chemist by profession and had joined the section 19 years ago. He had been promoted to his present job 14 years ago. Content with his lack of upward mobility, he had settled into a comfortable pattern of procrastination, feverish pattern of work activity, and a complete slowdown until the next project was initiated.

Perhaps as a result of Dorsey's contentment, the number of authorized employees in the section had remained static for the past five years. However, only two employees (Mr. Dorsey and Ms. Caldwell) had been in the department for over four years. The turnover rate for the past four years was over 70 percent. Oddly enough, three of the remaining employees were Mackell "lifers" having transferred from other areas of the company. Specifically, Perkins had 28 years service, Tabor was nearing 30 years service, and Jensen was approaching 15 years from two separate stints of employment. Of the two remaining employees, one had been with Mackell for two years (Groves), and the other (Whitt) had joined the company only six months ago. Given the constant state of change, the working climate of the section was one of confusion, stress, anxiety, and frustration.

In contrast, the information services section had grown rapidly in the preceding five years. In the past two years alone, three new positions had been created, for a total of 12 employees in the section. As a further contrast, the section had organized its human resources into four units—administration, R&D documents, micrographics, and library services—all reporting to the manager, Sharon Kastner. Although she had begun her career at the Mackell Company as a secretary, her aggressive behavior (she preferred to be labeled "assertive") had allowed her to rise rapidly through the ranks to her present position. Her often-voiced, self-admitted five-year plan was to become vice-president of STID. In order to accomplish this goal, she had begun expanding her control in an amoeba-like fashion. Just two years ago her section's primary (and only) function was to serve as a research library. By slowly building her power bases, she now duplicated much of the work being done in the information analysis section, whose work encompassed on-line search retrieval for medical topics, chemical topics, business topics, pharmacology topics, and topics of general interest. Under dubious pretenses, she had acquired access to several of the same database vendors as the information analysis section. By always having a reason, however nebulous, Mr. Dorsey had been coerced into allowing her access by Dr. Barton. Unable or unwilling to offer resistance, Mr. Dorsey had slowly diminished his responsibilities to that of a caretaker's role. He was now on the defensive and losing ground fast.

Throughout this timeframe Mr. Dorsey repeatedly voiced increased concern, both to individuals in the section as well as to the entire group. However, despite his repeated vows to "do something about the situation," procrastination reigned supreme. Section members were unsure whether he was deliberately relinquishing their duties, or if he was slowly losing his intuitive powers to senility. For example, one recent Friday afternoon, Mr. Dorsey, Mrs. Whitt, and Mrs. Groves were in a meeting concerning a particularly difficult search. As Mrs. Whitt was leaving on vacation, Mrs. Groves was going to be in charge during her absence. The following Monday morning Mrs. Groves approached Mr. Dorsey regarding the search and was shocked by his response.

Mr. Dorsey: I'm sorry, April, but I don't know what you're talking about.

April: Mr. Dorsey, remember the meeting we had Friday afternoon? We discussed the search tactics we would use and the parameters we would follow.

Mr. Dorsey: I'm drawing a total blank.

April: Mr. Dorsey, you took some notes during the meeting. Perhaps you put those in your desk drawer and that will refresh your memory.

Rummaging through his desk, Mr. Dorsey finally came upon a note pad that did indeed cover their meeting.

Mr. Dorsey: I certainly don't remember anything about this, but this is my handwriting. . . but are you sure that was Friday?

Situations such as this were common and had become a source of embarrassment for department members. Loyal to their manager, they tried to cover up for him whenever possible but often discussed the situation among themselves.

In recent months, the relationship between the information analysis section and the information services section had steadily deteriorated despite high-level managerial discussions of ways to resolve any conflict. The battle lines were drawn, and each group, led by its respective manager, was ready for combat. As an example of the strained relationship, Mrs. Harriett Grace (from the information services section) recently entered the office area of the information analysis section carrying an on-line printout of a patent citation. (Under the existing organizational scheme, patent searching was the responsibility of Mrs. April Groves in information analysis.) The following exchange occurred between Harriett, Sally Caldwell, and April.

Harriett: I would like to look up this patent in the books.

Sally: Well, you really should see April about that.

April: Harriett, did I hear you correctly? Just leave the patent and I will be happy to conduct a search for you.

Harriett: Oh, no. I want to do it myself.

April: There's the cabinet with the books, but as I said before, I will be glad to do it for you.

Refusing help, Harriett began pouring over the series of patent numbers arranged by accession numbers in volume upon volume of books. April almost giggled as she thought of Harriett mumbling to herself as she painstakingly searched each of the patent books. That outdated method had not been used since April joined the section almost two years ago. All of the searches that April conducted were on-line, using remote databases. The patent books were there only as a reminder of the past. While April laughed at Harriett's plight, Sally Caldwell fumed. In a brief glimpse, she had recognized the printout as one from a database whose access and use were limited to two people—herself and Alice Whitt. Knowing that neither she nor Mrs. Whitt had conducted a search on that topic, she finally could take it no longer and briskly walked to Mr. Dorsey's office. The door was closed, as usual. Knocking, she entered the room and began a verbal assault on Harriett and the entire information services section for attempting to take away her area of responsibility. Finally, Mr. Dorsey called April into his office to attempt to clarify the situation. The following conversation took place.

Mr. Dorsey: April, can you tell me why Harriett was looking for a patent?

April: No sir, but she had an abstract from a restricted database and requested permission to search the patent books. Mr. Dorsey, I'm sorry, but I couldn't bring myself to tell her that we did it online. I was afraid they would take that over also.

Mr. Dorsey: Well, I'm glad they don't know about *that,* but are you sure the citation was from the restricted database?

Sally: Mr. Dorsey, I need my job. You've got to do something about this situation. I do a good job and I don't appreciate their trying to take it over. There is something else they do that really bothers me. They are sending all of our reference requests to Sharon Kastner for review before filling them. Sharon gave me the third degree yesterday for doing a search that was on one of our products and she said that we are no longer authorized to do any product searches.

Mr. Dorsey: She did what? I've had it with this power struggle. You tell her that you're just doing your job, and if she has any questions, she can see me! Just refuse to talk to her!

As so often happened, Mr. Dorsey began a lengthy, derogatory exposé of Mrs. Kastner's character, her intentions, her political aspirations, and her close personal relationship with the director of STID. Meanwhile, as Mr. Dorsey drifted further and further off the subject in his rambling, both Mrs. Groves and Ms. Caldwell gave each other a knowing glance, knowing full well that this was the end of it; nothing more would be done.

QUESTIONS

1. Based on the dialogue, offer plausible explanations for the behavior of Mrs. Groves and Ms. Caldwell.

2. How could Mr. Dorsey be more effective in managing the conflict?

3. If top management made the decision to reorganize the two sections in an effort to alleviate the conflict, and you were chosen to develop a workable plan, outline the form of reorganization you would present to management.

33

FIRST AMERICAN BANK AND TRUST

First American Bank and Trust (FABT) was one of the largest banks in the state with over 120 offices in 40 communities. It was a subsidiary of First American Bankshares, Incorporated, a bank holding company headquartered in northern Virginia. A multibank holding company was formed in the early 1960s when nine banks combined resources of over $450 million. Acquisitions of a number of other banks continued throughout the years, and in the late 1970s the banks merged into their current status as a one-bank holding company. One reason for this merger was to provide a more favorable posture for entry into interstate banking once legislation was passed to allow this expansion. Today, FABT is a leading regional banking organization and is ranked in the top 200 banks nationally, with assets of almost $6 billion.

First American provides individual consumers, business, institutions, and governments with a broad range of services including international, trust, equipment leasing, and bank cards. Mortgage banking and investment advisory services are offered by the bank's wholly owned subsidiaries: First American Mortgage Service Corporation with 20 offices in six states; and American Investment Services, Incorporated, with three offices located throughout the state. In general, the bank is more commercially oriented than individual consumer-oriented.

THE TRUST GROUP

First American's trust services are provided by the trust group, which includes the subsidiary, American Investment Services, Incorporated. Services include financial planning, personal trust, pension trust, corporate trust, special trust services, and investment services. Depending on the particular item, trust services are offered at (up to) 10 locations throughout the state.

Currently the trust group is supported by a centralized trust service operations division, which is responsible for control, records, accounting, systems services, documentation and training, securities servicing, institutional services, and financial management. Prior to the one-bank merger, many of the trust operations functions were handled by each individual bank.

THE DILEMMA

Sue Barnette was delighted with her position as manager of the financial trust management department. After almost six years of work experience, she knew what she wanted in a job, and this position offered it all: challenge, autonomy, growth opportunity, and the ability to use a variety of skills.

Sue had initially interviewed for a senior financial analyst position, which had become vacant when the incumbent employee accepted another position in the bank. The interview had been with Bob Willison, manager of the department. This department consisted of three professional positions, including Bob's. Sue's second interview was with Rich Jacobs, division head of trust service operations and Bob's boss. During this interview, Rich discussed with Sue the opportunities available in the position, especially since Bob Willison was 63 years old. Instead of reporting to Bob, however, Sue would report directly to Rich, and the junior analyst in the department would report to her. Bob would continue to report to Rich, but only as a staff function. Rich also mentioned that the junior analyst, Martha Miller, had expressed an interest in the senior position. He did not feel, however, that her level of experience warranted the promotion. Sue was then offered the job and a few days later accepted the offer with unbridled enthusiasm.

During Sue's first weeks in the new position it appeared to her that Bob was unaware of the change in the reporting structure, although everyone else in the division seemed to know. Bob would pass along all of the correspondence that Rich had distributed to his immediate subordinates as if Sue had not seen it. He would also thoroughly question Sue about the content of her meetings with Rich. In addition, Bob would introduce Sue to others as Bill's replacement. Periodically, Bob would go into Sue's office, sit down, and begin talking. Basically, it was the same story each time.

> You know, before I joined the bank I was controller for a local moving firm here in town. When the business was sold, I came to the bank. That was fourteen years ago. Everybody in the control department, the records department, and the financial trust management department reported to me. Rich's secretary, Lucy, was my secretary—that is, when I still had one. That was before the one-bank merger. I used to have a real nice office—a nice, big wood desk, a wood credenza, a couple of side chairs and carpet on the floor—not this metal furniture like we have here now. The furniture up in Mr. Slocum's office used to be in mine—and he's head of the trust group! I've been thinking—since you and

Martha are taking a class this coming semester, I might, too. It would be in accounting—or something. I've picked up a catalogue.

Bob was well liked by everyone and had made many friends at the bank over the years, especially among the trust employees who had been with the bank when he was hired. His new responsibilities in the staff function consisted of preparing special analyses and reports, usually upon the request of Rich Jacobs or Mr. Slocum. In addition, Sue was told to feel free to utilize Bob's help whenever she needed it, although Bob was unaware of this function.

Three months after Sue began her job, Martha decided to accept another position in the bank. Her replacement was Jerry Donahue, a recent college graduate with no work experience other than summer jobs. Due to Jerry's lack of meaningful work experience, he required much guidance from Sue and could only perform routine, basic functions. Consequently, Sue temporarily assumed some of the responsibilities previously performed by Martha. About this same time, Rich was promoted to head up the corporate trust division as well as the trust service operations division.

Initially, Sue had requested Bob's help with some of the more complex tasks. She often found, however, that they were either incomplete or done incorrectly. As a result of this, and with Jerry's increasing proficiency, the tasks for which Sue requested Bob's assistance became more routine and less significant. In fact, the requests were often ignored or forgotten by Bob, and Jerry ended up doing the work.

Bob also started coming in to work late and taking long breaks and extended lunch hours. When he could be found in his office, he was often either staring out the window or talking to his wife on the telephone.

Gradually, more and more of the special requests began to go to Sue and Jerry.

Every two weeks Rich tried to hold one-on-one meetings with his immediate subordinates. During one of Sue's meetings with Rich the following conversation occurred.

Sue: Both Jerry and I have been working late and taking work home, but the work keeps piling up. We've been so busy trying to keep our heads above water, we haven't been able to devote any time to the long-range projects. We haven't even been able to start working on our goals for this year! Bob Willison hasn't been very helpful to us either. He always says he's working on a project for you or Mr. Slocum; then he spends the day looking out the window or running errands. Jerry has noticed this, too. Two people can only do the work of three for so long! I know senior management wants more analysis done than has been in the past. I really don't see any end in sight if things continue like this.

Rich: Bob will be 64 soon. When he retires we'll be able to hire someone who is capable of providing more assistance to you and Jerry. In the meantime, just continue to give Bob whatever work you can. I have another project for him, and he needs to do some more work on that last report he submitted to me. If I get some time, maybe I'll talk to him.

At that point, Lucy knocked on the door to remind Rich that it was time for his next appointment. It was not until later that evening when Rich had time to recall his conversation with Sue that he knew he had to do something—he just was not sure what that "something" should be.

QUESTIONS

1. Discuss the many ways in which Bob Willison's behavior can be considered disruptive to the trust group in general and to Sue's and Jerry's performance in particular.

2. What courses of action are available to Rich Jacobs that will correct the situation as it now exists?

34

STATE AUDITING OFFICE

Many years ago, the legislature of a state located on the eastern seaboard wanted assurance that financial transactions arising from legislation were handled properly. In order to accomplish this, the state auditing office was established as an agency under the legislature's control, with the state auditor being appointed by the legislature for a four-year term. The legislature could reappoint the state auditor for as many consecutive four-year terms as it deemed appropriate. The primary responsibility of the state auditor was to audit the various state agencies and governmental subdivisions in order to attest to the handling of revenues and expenditures in accordance with (1) the laws of the state; (2) the rules, regulations, and interpretations of authorized governmental bodies; and (3) the opinions of the Attorney General.

The state auditing office consisted of a central office located in the state capitol and five regional offices strategically located within the state. Staffing at the central office consisted of five secretaries, 40 staff auditors, five supervisors, an assistant state auditor, and the state auditor. Each of the regional offices had one supervisor and from six to 12 staff auditors.

Over the past 45 years this department operated in an extremely conservative manner:

1. Appointment to the position of state auditor normally came from within the state auditing office.

2. The staff size remained constant during the 45-year period, even though the size of the state government and the audit workload had increased tremendously.

3. The legislature changed the audit frequency for state agencies and allowed CPAs to audit some governmental subdivisions that were previously audited exclusively by the state auditing office.

4. Starting salaries lagged behind salaries paid by private industry or public accounting firms by $3000 to $5000.

5. Sometimes vacant staff auditor positions remained open for years because of low wages and the great amount of overnight travel required in certain regional offices.

6. Employee training programs and use of modern auditing techniques were rarely ever used.

7. Communication between the central office and the regional offices consisted primarily of memos from the state auditor to the staff auditors. The memos normally only outlined state code changes that affected state revenues and expenditures.

PERSONNEL CHANGES IN THE CENTRAL OFFICE

In 1981 the state auditor retired after serving two terms in the position and having a career with the state auditing office spanning 42 years. The legislature immediately appointed a new state auditor who, to the chagrin of many, was an outsider. Additionally, the new man was in his early thirties, had an MBA degree and CPA certification, but had only three years experience as an auditor. Shortly after the appointment, the assistant state auditor and two key supervisors in the central office retired. Thus, in the span of three months, four people retired who had a combined work experience of more than 160 years! A large public accounting firm was contracted immediately to perform a management services review of the state auditing office to recommend ways to improve the entire department. Shortly after the consultant's study had been completed, three additional people with CPA certification were hired. One was to fill the vacant assistant state auditor's position, and the other two were to manage supervisory-level personnel. Ironically, two of these individuals had participated in the major portion of the consulting firm's study. All of these people were in their late twenties.

Many changes resulted from the new management personnel and the report from the consultants:

1. Formal training programs were started.

2. Additional staff auditing positions were approved by the legislature.

3. Both starting salaries and upper-level salary ranges were increased.

At one of the all-day training sessions, attended by the entire staff of the rural regional offices, actual observation of the new management and of the reactions of the central office auditors were quite revealing to rural staff auditors.

MANAGEMENT LEADERSHIP PROBLEM

On the way home from the day-long training session, three of the rural staff auditors discussed the events of the day. Conversation centered on the following individuals: (1) Jack Logan, the current state auditor; (2) Arnold Crane, the current assistant state auditor; and (3) Joe Triplett, supervisor of rural regional offices.

Frank: What a Friday this has been! We are told to come to a training session that turns out to be a lecture, blasting us for doing a poor job. Then Arnold Crane gives us a pep talk on the new image of the state auditing office and how we have the opportunity to be a part of an organization that is on the way to becoming one of the best operating state agencies in the country.

John: Yes! And the next words from his mouth were, and I quote, "For those of you who are not willing to put forth the effort to become a part of the new image, there's the door."

Bill: Forget the hot air released at the training session. What do you think of the bomb shell just handed to us by Crane?

John: It doesn't surprise me that they are going to close our office and merge the region into the two adjoining regional offices and the central office. Two weeks ago, Joe Triplett attended a workshop held for supervisors. Apparently, Jack Logan and Arnold Crane discussed the consulting firm's recommendation of closing all regional offices and establishing another office similar to the central office in the western part of the state. In my opinion, the supervisors were able to convince them not to make any radical changes. However, with Mr. Triplett retiring in four months and only four staff auditors involved, our regional office is the easiest and most logical to close.

Bill: You're probably right, but the official reasons given to us for eliminating our regional office (not enough work and the expense of an underworked supervisor with only five people under him) just does not satisfy me. There are 12 counties that must be audited annually, and each county has three separate courts. In addition, there are three town audits, one county audit, two four-year colleges, three community colleges, a state hospital, 20 alcoholic beverage stores, and two city court systems!

John: Seven years ago our office had the responsibility of conducting two city audits and six county audits. However, unfilled vacancies made it impossible to do all the work, and many of the counties and both of the cities learned that Mr. Triplett was not qualified to do the job. As a result, we lost both city audits and five of the county audits. If we still had those jobs, we might be able to save our rural office.

Frank: At least they gave us some options regarding the closing of our office.

John: No, Mr. Crane told us what the options were! First, you don't have to move, but you have to work out of the eastern regional office, western regional office, or central office. In addition, you get mileage if you travel outside your county and room and board if you stay overnight. Second, if you elect to move in order to work in these offices, the state will pay the cost of moving. The options stink, in my opinion, because I am not going to move. I moved from the central office area to where I live now when I was hired. I asked to work in the central office and was told that the rural regional office was the only one with vacancies. I am not going to live out of a suitcase, which is the real meaning of the first option. The western office is 130 miles away; the eastern is 120 miles; and the central is 60 miles away. Perhaps the unmentioned but very real option of seeking employment elsewhere is for me. At least they gave us four months to make a decision.

Bill: I still cannot get over how afraid the central office staff auditors are of Arnold Crane.

John: If you were told on a daily basis, "You either do things my way or there's the door," you might be afraid, too; especially if you saw a couple of your buddies terminated! Perhaps the saddest thing in this whole situation is the method and means used by these new guys. The training sessions are needed; the auditing methods, procedures, and reports need to be changed; but the sad state of affairs did not occur overnight and they are not going to be cured overnight.

Frank: Mr. Crane strikes me as being power hungry, and now that he has some power, he wants to use it so everybody can see how powerful he is. The statement Mr. Crane made about Jack Logan doing what he told him to do reveals an overly self-confident attitude that is probably going to cause a confrontation between the two of them sometime in the future.

John: In the meantime, the older men in their late forties, fifties, and early sixties who were hired to do certain aspects of auditing such as adding a bunch of receipt books, counting the bottles in a liquor store, or other such menial auditing work will suffer because now they are expected to change from what they have been doing for 20 years. Now they are expected to know how to write an audit program, to audit using statistical samples, and to organize work papers in a standard coded way.

Frank: What do you think Mr. Crane meant by saying that pay raises will be based primarily on merit?

John: I'm not sure, but I do remember once when Mr. Triplett decided to evaluate one auditor so poorly that no raise was given for two straight years. When the third year came and the rating was still poor, the state personnel office told Mr. Triplett to either fire the guy or give him a better rating. The same will probably occur here. However, I like the idea of paying the better performer a higher wage than the person who is just putting in time.

Bill: One thing that I don't like is being talked down to, as though I am unable to comprehend what is happening. John, you and I have talked about many of the things they plan to do in the next 12 months, such as training sessions, statistical sampling, standardized work papers, merit pay, and so forth. They have not provided us a mechanism to voice our opinion on needed changes, such as more timely updates on state code changes and changes in federal programs.

John: Right now, the state auditing office is following the report of the consultant, which proposes a four-year program for implementing recommended changes. Logan and his managers and assistant do not want input from the workers.

The rest of the trip back to the rural regional office was marked by silence as each person contemplated his future with the state auditing office under the new leadership.

QUESTIONS

1. Based on the background and dialogue, who appears to be currently running the state auditing office? How would you describe this individual's leadership style?

2. Based on the information presented, discuss the aspects of stress, motivation, and communication as each relates to this situation.

35

ANDREW WHITMORE AND COMPANY, INC.

$\mathbf{A}$ndrew Whitmore and Company, Inc. is an old and well-established public accounting firm with offices throughout the East and Southeast. From its headquarters in Atlanta, Georgia, Whitmore establishes policies and procedures regarding the most efficient accounting technology for use in all offices for performance comparison purposes. In addition, all significant personnel policies and practices originate from Atlanta and are based on recommendations from various central planning committees. However, each Whitmore branch office is allowed considerable latitude in the implementation of personnel policies and is also treated as a separate profit center.

WASHINGTON OFFICE

One of Whitmore's most profitable offices is in Washington, D.C. Due to a highly competent staff as well as a prime location, the Washington office has made consistant and significant contributions to the overall organization profit picture. Over the past 10 years, this particular office has been ranked among the top five Whitmore branches in terms of profit and number of clients served.

In addition to 12 partners, Washington employs a professional staff of about 120 individuals. Members of the staff are classified on the basis of their level of experience. Specifically, those employees designated simply as staff are the youngest and largest group with typically two to three years of experience before attaining senior status. The seniors are eligible for promotion to manager after their total experience reaches five to six years. Finally, after managers have 10 to 12 years of experience, they become eligible for partner status.

TURNOVER PROBLEMS

Whereas Andrew Whitmore and Company has always experienced steady turnover at all levels of its professional staff, the firm actually views *some* turnover as desirable. In periods of moderate business growth, a high ratio of staff to partners can be maintained while still promoting all capable employees only if some attrition occurs. At the present time, however, the professional staff in Washington has been losing its depth and experience as more and more seniors are quitting despite good or excellent performance evaluations. Consequently, managers have been forced to get involved in details that normally would be delegated downward. Morale has been falling quickly as the reduced senior level staff has created greater overtime commitments for everyone.

Clients in the Washington area have also been complaining about the greater time they need to devote to audit engagements because of Whitmore's inability to use the same senior personnel on repeat engagements. This has required the clients to acquaint new senior staff members with their accounting records. It is apparent that the firm has been losing too many of its senior staff to operate efficiently, and some action has to be taken in the near future to avoid any additional customer complaints.

A SENIOR'S PERSPECTIVE

"How am I supposed to get anything done in here," thought Doug Hartnett as he tried to ignore the phone discussion of Ned Wilson and the adding machine rattle of Joyce Rudnay, two senior staff members who shared a cramped office with Doug.

"I'm really getting tired of this," Doug's thoughts continued as he reviewed the audit workpapers his staff has prepared. "I've been with this firm for four years and I'm still expected to make sure that another accountant who only has two years experience can move a number from page A-47 to page A-35 without miscopying it." His thoughts went on as he slammed shut the Mendelson Company workpapers file and reached for their draft financial statements.

"Well, if you ask me," Doug overheard Ned saying into the phone, "manager is about the worst position in this firm. New managers have to hang around six years hoping to make partner and 75 percent of them never make it. Further, not only do they not make partner, but those six years experience really add nothing to their marketability with another organization and they find they are overpriced for other jobs. If you don't make partner you're better off never having stayed to find out. I can't believe that with those odds all those managers were honestly counseled about their opportunities with the firm. The partners just needed somebody to be a manager and they know no one would stay unless they received pretty high performance evaluations."

Doug reached for some tape to secure a section of the draft financial statements the partner had deleted from note 5 and wanted moved to note 3. As he lined up the note on the paper, his mind began to wander. "I

309

don't know why I always get these small clients. I was hoping I'd get one of the large clients in the office, but I guess they're reserved for those who are really doing well."

"Hey, Doug," called Ned as Doug headed out the office door.

"Let me get you later, Ned," returned Doug. "I have to get these financials up to Sam Watkins. We are going to lunch to review my performance on the Mendelson audit and the financial statement disclosures and then discuss the audit with the client."

Doug headed up the long corridor to "Partners' Row." He didn't like all the details he had to follow through on, but there was a sense of satisfaction in knowing he had done a good job. Sam Watkins should be pleased.

"Mr. Watkins can't be disturbed," offered his secretary as Doug readied his hand to knock on the door. "He has to prepare for testimony he's giving later this week before the Securities and Exchange Commission," she continued. "He did ask that you leave the Mendelson financial statements with me so he can discuss them with the client later today," she concluded.

"Sure," Doug replied. "Why not?"

A PARTNER'S PERSPECTIVE

Sam Watkins liked the feel of the oriental carpet under his feet as he walked into his office at 7:30 a.m. Monday morning. The carpet was such a nice contrast with the commercial carpeting used in the outer hallway. He switched on his office light, and the sight of the Chippendale furnishings, oriental wall hangings and oversized partner's desk still made him smile with the thought, "Yes, I have arrived."

Sam checked his calendar. At 9:00 he was to meet with an audit committee to review an audit plan for a Fortune 500 client. At noon, he and Doug Hartnett were going to discuss the Mendelson engagement and financial statements. Later that afternoon he was to prepare testimony for the Securities and Exchange Commission on an accounting issue. "Damn," he thought. "I've procrastinated on that testimony too long already. I'd better push Mendelson back a while. I'll reschedule it for tomorrow and tell my secretary to notify Doug Hartnett."

Sam checked the next office to see if Dan Benner, another partner in the Washington office, was in yet, but he was not. Dan's close proximity was the result of one of the features that Sam enjoyed most about the office layout. All of the partners' offices were clustered at the southern end of the building. The layout originally was designed to take advantage of the best view from the building, but as a result, the partners' offices were much more quiet and secluded from the traffic of other areas. A separate kitchen and bathroom for the partners' exclusive use had also evolved.

Sam returned to his desk, but before he could sit down, the personnel status sheets in his in-basket caught his eye. Sam normally felt quite at ease in the technical problems of his accounting work. But the turnover problems highlighted on the personnel status sheets were concerns with which he felt much less comfortable.

In his own mind, Sam viewed the firm's primary attraction for seniors as the opportunity for growth. To those for whom a career in public accounting was appealing, the prestige and opportunities available at Whitmore were unmatched even by most of its peers. And with an average partner salary in excess of

$150,000, the financial rewards were significant. In addition, even for those seniors who could not or who chose not to become partners with the firm, the experience they acquired was valuable and could springboard them into many other careers as well.

Other partners in the Washington office seemed convinced that the solution to the senior staff's high rate of turnover was additional salary. They noted that, on the average, seniors indicated raises of 15 to 20 percent in salary as reasons for leaving the firm, and the only way to stem the tide was to grant an immediate increase in the salary structure.

Sam was still undecided about what steps the firm should take. Sam asked the personnel manager to prepare a summary of current professional salaries. Within a week, Sam Watkins received the information. The breakdown on salaries was as follows:

Level	Experience	Salary
Staff	1–3 years	$15,000– $20,999
Seniors	2–5 years	$21,000– $29,999
Managers	5–12 years	$30,000– $45,000
Partners	10 years or more	$70,000–$250,000

After reviewing the figures, Sam thought everyone else was correct, and a revamping of Whitmore's salary structure required top priority. Surely this would curb their turnover problem, Sam later commented to one of the partners.

QUESTIONS

1. What motivational factors are the partners of Andrew Whitmore and Company ignoring in their proposal to raise salaries of seniors in order to decrease their turnover?

2. Discuss possible courses of action that Whitmore could undertake to resolve their unacceptable level of turnover. How would these courses of action correct the motivational problems?

36

SPECIALTY GIFTS, INC.

"We only thought we had troubles last week," Jim Johnson explained to his wife. "Danish Imports just notified us that any further orders we place with them must be accompanied by a check for the entire amount of the order." It was February, 1982.

Jim and Hilda Johnson were the owners of Specialty Gifts, Inc., which was located in a large Mid-Atlantic metropolitan area. Danish Imports was the second vendor that had discontinued their credit line for purchasing merchandise. Even worse, 35 percent of Specialty Gifts' merchandise was provided by these two vendors. Compounding the problem was the fact that the slowest sales period of the year would soon arrive, and Specialty Gifts would also need to begin placing orders for merchandise to be delivered in the fall. There was little cash available, and it appeared as though vendor credit would be limited.

COMPANY BACKGROUND

Specialty Gifts, Inc. was formed in May 1977 and located in an ocean-front store in the resort section of the metropolitan area. The store's merchandise consisted of trendy and inexpensive gift items targeted primarily toward tourists. After a year, the operation was relocated to another ocean-front store and for two years

Case prepared by Walter Riggs, Management Department, Georgia State University and reprinted with permission.

proved to be increasingly profitable. However, the owners felt that business was too dependent on the often erratic tourist trade.

In 1980, a second store was opened at a shopping center in a relatively high median income section of the resort city. Accordingly, the product line offered at this store was modified. Relatively expensive specialty gift items such as gourmet cooking utensils, linen napkins and tablecloths, and unusual glassware became the mainstay. The new store proved to be extremely profitable.

Due to the success of the new store, the owners decided to open a third store in early 1981. The location chosen was a soon-to-be opened shopping mall in another city within the metropolitan area. This particular location was chosen with the objective of capturing another segment of the market.

Both of the owners were college graduates in their late twenties. Jim Johnson had had three years of retailing experience with Sears, Roebuck and Company. His wife, Hilda, had been a home economics teacher prior to her involvement in the Specialty Gifts venture.

THE MARKET

The parent store was located in a large resort suburb that was experiencing one of the fastest population growth rates on the East Coast. It also had one of the highest median incomes in the region. Due to the influx of new industry and increased concentration of state and federal personnel these conditions would probably continue.

In addition, the original location in the resort area had a 100-day tourist season that drew visitors from the affluent cities of the East. It was advertised that the resort was within a one-day's drive from all the major eastern metropolitan areas. Approximately 1.5 million overnight tourists visited the area each year.

The new store was to be opened in a shopping mall in a neighboring city. This city was primarily a blue-collar industrial town whose population had a median income approximately 25 percent less than that of the resort city. The owners felt, however, that the lack of competition and the drawing ability of the mall would make the location successful. The product line was to be the same as that of the parent store.

THE EVENTS OF 1981

Jim and Hilda Johnson began 1981 with great antici-pation. During the spring, they made several buying trips to both foreign and domestic suppliers. A large quantity of merchandise was ordered during these trips. The orders were to be delivered sometime around Labor Day.

Most of the Specialty Gifts vendors provided rela-tively liberal credit terms for payment of goods that were shipped. It was a frequent vendor practice to allow 90 days for payment, particularly during the Christ-mas season. However, the suppliers expected that all invoices would be paid soon after the Christmas shop-ping season.

The new shopping mall was scheduled to open on September 1, 1981. However, due to construction de-lays it did not open until November 1, thus resulting in a very short fall shopping season. In addition, the traf-fic in the mall itself was only about half of that which was anticipated. This was attributed to the effect of

	1979	1980	1981*
Net Sales	$133,500	$233,500	$389,000
Cost of Goods Sold	82,700	126,000	198,100
Gross Profit	50,800	107,500	190,900
EXPENSES			
Salaries	12,800	26,180	74,291
Utilities	2,030	2,920	5,640
Rent	8,500	15,660	31,180
Supplies	1,100	2,870	7,380
Advertising	600	4,400	8,000
Travel	690	1,430	1,170
Other expenses	2,250	1,890	12,822
Net income before tax	22,830	52,150	50,417
Income tax			10,906
Net income after tax	22,830	52,150	39,511

*Specialty Gifts became a corporation during 1981 and the officers were paid a salary of $17,400 during the year.

FIGURE 36.1   Specialty Gifts, Inc. income statement (three years ending December 31, 1981)

declining economic conditions, which adversely affected blue collar workers.

At the end of the year, the Johnsons' accountant prepared all of their financial statements (as shown in Figures 36.1 and 36.2) and spent the better part of a day reviewing all technical matters relevant to their finances. At this point, the Johnsons were deeply concerned about the excess merchandise that was on hand. Almost all of this inventory was to have been sold in the new mall location. However, the short selling season and less than anticipated traffic at this location had been the major cause of their dilemma. Nevertheless, the Johnsons had to do something to preserve their business and they had to do something quick.

	1979	1980	1981*
Current assets			
Cash	$10,000	$12,500	$ 2,900
Accounts receivable	4,800		13,100
Inventory	11,800	46,000	212,000
Total current assets	26,600	58,500	228,000
Fixed assets			
Equipment (less accu-			
mulated depre.)	11,500	15,500	41,000
Leasehold improve-	2,500	25,300	58,500
ment			
Truck (less accumulat-			
ed depreciation)			4,500
Total fixed assets	14,000	40,800	104,000
Total assets	$40,600	$99,300	$332,000
Current liabilities			
Notes payable	$10,000	$ 2,300	$ 27,000
Vendors payable			128,000
Total current liabilities	10,000	2,300	155,000
Long-term liabilities			
Loans payable	6,600	46,900	110,000
Total long-term liabilities	6,600	46,900	110,000
Owners equity			
Common stock			5,500
Net worth	24,000	50,100	61,500
Total liabilities and			
owners equity	$40,600	$99,300	$332,000

*Specialty Gifts became a corporation during 1981.

FIGURE 36.2   Specialty Gifts, Inc. balance sheet (three
years ending December 31, 1981)

QUESTIONS

1. What errors in planning did Jim and Hilda make when locating the new store?

2. What should the Johnsons have done when it was determined that the mall opening was going to be delayed?

3. What might the owners do at this point to save the business?

658 Ash
Ashworth, D. Neil.
Cases in management : examining critical

CAPE FEAR COMMUNITY COLLEGE

3 3177 00063 4110